Changing the World
THROUGH MEDIA EDUCATION

Changing the World
THROUGH MEDIA EDUCATION

Part of Developing Minds™
A New Media Literacy Curriculum
by the Just Think Foundation

Elana Yonah Rosen
Arli Paulin Quesada
Sue Lockwood Summers

fulcrum resources
Golden, Colorado

Dedicated to teachers, who make a difference in all our lives.

Copyright © 1998 Just Think Foundation

Book design by Deborah Rich
Cover art © 1998 Sheryl Chapman, Kelly Clark, Laura Mitchell
Inside art/icons © 1998 Kelly Clark, Craig Halsted Hannah

Library of Congress Cataloging–in–Publication Data
  Rosen, Elana Yonah.
      Changing the World through media education / by Elana Yonah Rosen, Arli Paulin Quesada, Sue Lockwood Summers.
          p.   cm. – (Developing minds)
      "A new media literacy curriculum by the Just Think Foundation." Includes bibliographical references and index.
      ISBN 1-55591-971-5 (pbk.)
      1. Audio–visual education–Handbooks, manuals, etc. 2. Audio–visual materials–Handbooks, manuals, etc. 3. Media literacy–Handbooks, manuals, etc. 4. Mass media–Study and teaching (Middle school)–Handbooks, manuals, etc. 5. Critical thinking–Study and teaching (Middle school)–Handbooks, manuals, etc. 6. Curriculum planning–Handbooks, manuals, etc. I. Quesada, Arli Paulin. II. Summers, Sue Lockwood. III. Just Think Foundation. IV. Title. V. Series.
      LB1043.R66   1998
      371.33'5–dc21   97–44906
                                                                                    CIP

Printed in the United States of America
0 9 8 7 6 5 4 3 2

Fulcrum Publishing
16100 Table Mountain Parkway, Suite 300
Golden, Colorado 80403
(800) 992-2908 • (303) 277-1623
www.fulcrum-resources.com

Permissions/Copyright Information

Tom Ostlund, 1992, referenced by David Haury and Peter Rillero (p. 113) in "Perspectives of Hands-On Science Teaching" (ERIC Clearinghouse for Science, Mathematics and Environmental Education, 1994). Permission granted by Robert Michael Esformes, editor, *INQUIRY*.

Wendy Oxman (p. 118), "Critical Thinking as Creativity," *INQUIRY: Critical Thinking Across the Disciplines*, vol. 9, no. 3 (Institute for Critical Thinking, April 1992). Permission granted by Wendy Oxman.

"Project-Based Learning: An Effective Approach" (p. 118), (Global School Net Foundation, 1995), cdweb@gsn.org. Permission granted by Global School Net Foundation.

"Project Design Process" (pp. 111 & 121), developed by Ross Valley School District, San Anselmo, California, in collaboration with Autodesk Foundation, www.autodesk.com/foundation. Reprinted with permission of the Autodesk Foundation and Ross Valley School District. For further information, visit the Autodesk Foundation website at: www.autodesk.com/foundation.

Nora Redding (p. 112), "Assessing the Big Outcomes," *Educational Leadership*, vol. 49, no. 8 (Association for Supervision and Curriculum Development, May 1992). Copyright © 1992 by ASCD. Reprinted by permission. All rights reserved.

Sally Smith (p. 109), "Educating the Learning Disabled for the Future," *Their World* (National Center for Learning Disabilities, 1992). Permission granted by Janet Weinstein, NCLD.

Kendall Starkweather (p. 134), International Technology Education Association (ITEA) keynote address at Autodesk Foundation's Midwinter Conference on Project-Based Education, 1994. Permission granted by Kendall Starkweather.

Terry Thode as quoted by Arli Quesada (p. 118) in "A Mind Set for the Future," *The Technology Teacher* (International Technology Education Association, October 1995). Permission granted by Kathleen Sheehan, editor, *The Technology Teacher*, ITEA.

Paulette Thomas (p. 4), "Show and Tell: Advertisers Take Pitches to Preschools," *The Wall Street Journal* (October 28, 1996), pp. B1, B5. Reprinted by permission of *The Wall Street Journal* © 1996, Dow Jones & Company, Inc. All Rights Reserved Worldwide.

David Walsh, Ph.D., Larry S. Goldman, Ph.D., and Roger Brown, Ph.D. (pp. 3 & 6), *Physician Guide to Media Violence*, American Medical Association, © 1996. And E. B. White quoted in David Walsh, Ph.D., Larry S. Goldman, Ph.D., and Roger Brown, Ph.D. (p. 3). *Physician Guide to Media Violence*, American Medical Association, © 1996.

Thomas Watson Jr. and Peter Petre (p. 184), *Father, Son & Co.: My Life at IBM and Beyond* (New York: Bantam Books, 1990). Permission granted by Bantam Books, a division of Doubleday Dell Publishing Group.

John Nasbitt in Richard Saul Wurman (p. 184), *Information Anxiety: What to Do When Information Doesn't Tell You What You Need to Know.* (New York: Bantam Books, 1989). Permission granted by Bantam Books, a division of Doubleday Dell Publishing Group.

Contents

Foreword

Our children are growing up in an ever-changing world that is vastly different from when we were young. Some of this change can be attributed to the growing demands placed on families by work, a rapidly evolving economy, or changes in the family structure. Certainly, one undeniable change is the influence of popular culture and the media.

So now more than ever, our schools and teachers face the unique challenge of educating our children for the twenty-first century. This is a basic but often overlooked step to begin preparing children to understand popular culture.

Popular culture is created through the messages we read in magazines, newspapers, and billboards; messages we see in movies, on TV, and now from the expanding Information Superhighway–the Internet and interactive media.

That is why this book is so important.

These new forms of communication have made messages more persuasive than ever. Thus, our children must develop critical thinking skills, or "media literacy," which will enable them to evaluate and understand the effect that media has on their lives. To begin this process, we must give teachers, community leaders, and parents the tools to help children better understand the daily barrage of messages.

This book on media education contains inspirational messages from children who shared their own innovative and fresh ideas about global communications with six hundred children from forty countries in Paris, France, during the Annual Children's Summit. Ten of these children attended the summit in Paris in 1996, another thirteen students represented North America in 1997, while thousands of others participated virtually–online and via e-mail. Some even chose to use the more traditional U.S. Postal Service.

These bright and gifted children, whom I had the honor of hosting on Capitol Hill in Washington, D.C., are the inspiration for this book to help teachers, parents, and other children better understand solutions for the future. They astutely address the pressing issues of our time: violence, racism, concern for the environment, self-esteem, and communications. Most important, they serve as models for young people who wish to understand and use media to invent their own powerful messages.

With thoughtful consideration and integration of the lessons in this book into schools, communities, and homes, our children can begin to develop the life skills needed to analyze, evaluate, and understand the media that shape their everyday lives.

Representative Tim Roemer
Member of Congress

Preface

The Just Think Foundation was established to stimulate critical thinking about popular media. The foundation examines how and why traditional and interactive media affect young people. By understanding the media that surround us, we believe young people will make better decisions every day and develop the new literacy skills critical for tomorrow.

The way Just Think fulfills these goals is by producing provocative Public Service Announcements (PSAs) encouraging kids to think about the impact of media around them. We also design educational curricula to equip young people with literacy tools vital for the future. The PSAs the foundation creates accompany TV shows, films, CD–ROMs, and online sites with positive messages to spark awareness about the content of media. The media literacy programs Just Think produces provide resources for students, teachers, and parents in schools and community centers. Just Think is working with educational organizations and the entertainment industry to let kids know that the movies they see or video games they play can be extremely entertaining but are not always a model for behavior. If young people "just think" about the meaning of messages that surround them, research shows they are less likely to "just act" upon violent, sexist, or racist models.

This teacher curriculum guide is the first nonelectronic publication in a series called "Developing Minds." Developing Minds is a set of resources composed of a curriculum guide for teachers, a guidebook for parents, a comic book for students, videotapes, and a CD–ROM for classrooms or community centers. It is intended for students of fourth through eighth grades and can be easily extended to older children. Whether you are wired or not, in school or in the community, Just Think offers research and resources to bring media education to your district, town, or city.

Acknowledgments

The goals for this book were conceived during breakfast at Mama's Royal Cafe in Mill Valley, California, when Aaron Singer and I first discussed what was most important to us: how new media were affecting young people. It was at that table that Just Think was born, and with the fire of Aaron's creativity and intuition, it will endure. Thank you to Megan Wheeler and Aaron for providing the nest of The ad•hoc Group from which the Just Think Foundation has taken flight. Without their support and the interest of ad•hoc's entire staff, it would have been impossible to launch the foundation, let alone accomplish what we have since May 1995.

Enormous thanks to Arli Paulin Quesada and Jill Brody, who took the great leap into the classroom with me to design and pilot Developing Minds, which became the basis for the curriculum guide you hold. Without their extraordinary commitment, intelligence, faith, and trust in creating this program, our first set of students at Martin Luther King/Bayside and Northbay Schools in Sausalito and Marin City, California, would not have produced their first CD-ROM with incredibly inspiring and powerful messages about education, self-esteem, the environment, the consequences of drugs and violence, and the importance of friendship for others to see and hear.

Thank you, Arli, for developing the tie between project-based learning and new media literacy with me as described in Step 3 of this workbook. And a special thanks to Arli for always being the string to my balloon.

Thank you, Sue Lockwood Summers, for your ability to crystallize your experience of seventeen years teaching media literacy into meaningful and pertinent experiences for students and teachers alike. Many thanks for developing the key issues and activities in Step 2.

Thank you to teachers Cybil Cox and Mattie Knighten for sharing their students with us for our first pilot programs. Thanks to principals Peggy Hirsch and Steve Port for letting us drag equipment and all forms of media into the classroom and take their students out to explore yet another world of new media.

It is with gratitude that I thank Representative Tim Roemer for his everlasting words and unmatched commitment toward the health and well-being of all children.

Thanks to Samantha Davidson and Milton Chen for KQED's active support of Developing Minds and providing Laura Hodder to research a great number of the video resources listed in the back of this book.

Thank you to Pepa Gonzalez, Jean Holzgang, Wendy Hysko, Jessica Minier Mabe, and Nicole Wagenberg of the Just Think Foundation who have been the everyday life support system for this book.

Many thanks to interns Ian Reyes and Jeremy Sharrard who posted quotes by students from the International Children's Summit on Just

Think's website every week. Many of the extraordinary ideas from these young people are included in this book. A special thanks to Diana Alden Lang, Heather Angney, Steward Bennett, Beverly Carruth, Michel Fraser, Nina Giglio, Roby Gilbert, Steve Heard, Daphne Humes, Raynetta James, Glen Janssens, Aaron Kilber, Paul Lundahl, Meredith Shuwall, Matthew Simpson–Stratton, and Rob Tsuyuki whose volunteer work exceeded all expectations and sustained Just Think during our founding year.

There will never be enough ways to thank Jan D'Alessandro Wadsworth who incorporated the Just Think Foundation. Jan has vivaciously and voraciously evangelized Just Think during her every waking hour (not to mention bringing new meaning to all preconceived ideas about lawyers).

Thank you, Chuck Champlin, whose heart and mind brought Just Think into the partnership that resulted in cohosting the 3rd and 4th Annual International Children's Summit in Paris, France. Chuck catapulted the Foundation into an international arena, and it is with Chuck's ongoing support that Just Think continues to encourage media education locally, nationally, and internationally.

A particularly deep thank you to our first sponsors, the Packard Foundation, the Sobrato Family Foundation, America Online, and Disney.

Thanks to Rachel Gaunt, who brings wit and wisdom to the challenging balance between advertisement and education. And thanks to Just Think's board of advisors, particularly Richard Wolpert and Tom Luddy who always find time to answer my questions while lending insight. Deborah Goldblatt's expert advice has been invaluable from the beginning production of this book through the final draft.

Thanks to the Marin City Community Project participants for their excellent questions and important feedback ensuring that Just Think's programs extend out from the school into the community and beyond.

A big thank you to Sheryl Chapman, Kelly Clark, Craig Halsted Hannah, and Laura Mitchell for their artistic contributions and ongoing dedication to Just Think.

Many thanks to Suzanne Barchers and Alison Auch whose knowledge of the subject matter made editing conference calls a stimulating event, whose sensitivity to language is extremely fine, and whose enthusiasm about teaching and learning provides a model for all. Thank you to Bob Baron and Carol Clark of Fulcrum Publishing who brought me in like a member of their family and continue to treat me as such.

An important thank you to Roz Kirby who has modeled goals for me to aspire to in the classroom and the workplace. She reminds me that a great idea and a sound sense of integrity should never be compromised, particularly in the context of the future of our children.

And thanks to my wild and wondrous parents, siblings, and most unusual extended family, all of whom have inspired and invigorated me through every step of my life.

Elana Yonah Rosen
Cofounder and Executive Director, Just Think Foundation

INTRODUCTION

"If I could send a message ... it would be to ask questions about EVERYTHING! Be content and happy in who you are! Don't live for others ... respect yourself ... never look down on those less fortunate than yourself. If I had access to all the technologies in the world ... I would use them all to reach as many people as I could. Not everyone has an Internet account or a movie house or perhaps even a boombox to listen to. The next best thing would be to live the 'message' through my life, because even if you were blind or deaf, I could hold your hand and guide your steps through the many obstacles we encounter each day."

W. Biermen (age unknown)
Oakland, California

If you could send a *message* to all your students, what would it be? In 1996, the Just Think Foundation asked young people what kind of message they would send to children around the world, and how they would say it. Fifteen thousand children wrote and e-mailed us their insightful ideas. A taste of their work is interspersed throughout this book. We found our students were inspired by great work from other students, as were we. We hope you find their quotes similarly helpful to you and your students in finding the best use of "new media literacy" in your classroom.

What Is New Media Literacy?
Let's start with the parts. To see something clearly, an insightful teacher might suggest looking at it in a new way. In this case, try looking at the trio of words backwards. That would be–*literacy, media,* and *new.*

Webster's defines *literacy* as the state of being literate, and literate as "(1a) characterized by or possessed of learning: Educated, cultured."[1]

Many educators consider the concept of critical thinking a basic literacy. "Learning to think critically is an essential and powerful vehicle for developing literacy abilities and in constructing knowledge at every level of education."[2] This was well summarized by Dr. George Hanford, professor emeritus, the College Board: "An education based on the knowledge of facts without the wisdom to interpret them is a hollow deception ... critical thinking is essential to both effective learning and productive living."[3]

Next, to clarify matters, refer back to *Webster's. Media* is the plural of *medium*, "(3) something through or by which something is accomplished, conveyed or carried on."[4]

We all think we know what media are. More often than not, when we think of media, we think of TV. Think a bit more: Media are newspapers, books, comics, magazines, bumper stickers, T–shirts, billboards, radio, music *CDs* ... keep thinking ... magnets on refrigerators, logos on running shoes, high–fashion designs, and as the *interactive* world expands, media include video games, *CD-ROMs*, *Internet* sites, and *virtual realities (VR)*.

In the context of this book consider for a moment the word *message* to be very closely synonymous with *media*. Although Marshall McLuhan argued that the medium is the message,[5] this teacher's guide will em–phatically plead that the *medium is not necessarily the message*. The message is the message and is defined more or less powerfully according to which medium is used and in what way it is conveyed. Which is very much what this book is about.

Now Explore the "New" Part for a Moment

"New" has lots of implications. Fresh, modern, novel ... untested ... and for some teachers, burdensome. But when paired with media, its reference is specific. It doesn't just encompass video games, CD-ROMs, online sites, and VR worlds. *New media* are interactive and hence imply interaction–you answer questions, play games, navigate paths, and explore environments (using the remote to switch channels on the TV doesn't count). It assumes a two–way exchange and therefore is pedagogically more profound because it embraces active learning. Research also supports the potential for *constructivist* learning through interactive media.

Breaking Down and Building Up Concepts

So, new media literacy is possessing learning skills about thinking criti–cally and conveying messages in a variety of forms. That is what we mean. And did you notice ... very simply, and very quickly, we just *deconstructed, analyzed,* and interpreted a term. That process is also what this book is really about, and it is from here we will begin.

Look back to look ahead.

In the 1960s, media literacy emerged as the ability to interpret, analyze, reflect upon, deconstruct, understand, *evaluate,* and *construct* media in varied forms. The concept is not new, but the reality of the effect of new media is. The stories haven't changed much from the days of radio and early TV, but our experiences with media have changed dramatically.

Popular culture is now defined by the avalanche of media depicting everything from the all-star–priced shoes that will make us champions, to diet–till–you–drop drinks that will make us popular, to the deluge of media entertainment in which we engage.

I believe television is going to be the test of the modern world, and that in this new opportunity to see beyond the range of our vision we shall discover either a new and unbearable disturbance of the general peace or a saving radiance in the sky. We shall stand or fall by television.[6]

E. B. White, 1938

Why Integrate Media?

The American Medical Association reports in *AMA, 1996* that children spend more than twice as much time each year learning from media as they do from the combined time with parents and teachers.[7] *Twice* as much time. This is striking.

Media have grown in force with popular culture, while schools have caught the second wave. As technologies are developed to control the entertainment industry, teachers must equip themselves with an understanding of media to be used as effective tools for teaching. While young people embraced media, many schools, initially, did not. However, schools can use their students' interest in media to teach all subjects, approach sensitive issues, and solve complex problems.

Cybil Cox, a middle school teacher at Martin Luther King/Bayside School in California, noticed her students were walking around the playground imitating the "goose step" reminiscent of Nazi Germany. She recounted a textbook history unit linking their walk with the origin of that march to help the children understand why some people would find it offensive. Her students were not grasping the connection. Then she showed a *documentary* demonstrating Hitler's army in the context of his attempt to annihilate a population of people. Her students were captured by the footage. Because they were taken in by the medium, they discovered that the topic did indeed pertain to the behavior they mimicked and understood how it could be interpreted or possibly misinterpreted. Only then did they begin to acquire the information they needed to see the relevance of the subject at hand.

Many children's interests have tumbled away from school, and a substantial part of the reason is media. We can judge for ourselves when we think the content is good or bad, but to deny its force outside and inside the classroom is potentially harmful to students.

We might never have predicted this change would come but, as educators, we know it's time to embrace media and new technology as additional teaching tools. It's crucial not only because of historically predictable problems that will arise in our *society* if the abyss between those students with new tools and those without deepens, but our students of today will not be able to function in any workplace of tomorrow. They must develop the skills necessary for the future, and it is our job as educators and parents to know enough about these skills to teach them to our students and children.

In facing the future, we know that the education *community* and the information and entertainment industries must work together.

Participation of children in media prepares students for lifelong exposure to media. For very young students this means understanding the difference between fantasy and reality, so three year olds don't knock each other out cold in the sandbox. For older students it's understanding that Michael Jordan may be the "super-coolest" sports figure of the end of the twentieth century, but he doesn't necessarily know which shoe fits you best, nor does he tell you which will last longest (not to mention whether they'll help you make it to the NBA). It means comprehending the values expressed by a rap artist who meets success and responds to it by perpetuating *violence*, racial indignation, and sexual abuse versus the values of one who does not. And more to the point, it means providing young people with the tools to make informed decisions every day to guarantee success for the rest of their lives.

There are many reasons why this new literacy is vital for your students: The quantity and quality of messages students now receive through the print media has increased; the introduction of the Internet provides easier access to a variety of messages; societal changes in family structure, new priorities, lifestyles, and schedules leave less time for interaction between children and parents. Yet another reason has to do with the *marketing* strategies now used to target young people. Cover Concepts Marketing Services is targeting preschoolers by sending product samples, coupons, and coloring books to twenty-two thousand daycare centers in exchange for demographic data sold to McDonalds and Kellogg's.[8]

Another rationale for teaching media literacy is related to risky behaviors that can be directly or indirectly connected to media messages, such as alcohol and tobacco use. For these reasons, it is time to help students be analytical and media savvy. In addition, media-related career choices may encourage students to stay in school and become tomorrow's media makers (see Appendix B, p. 155)

These are a few reasons why this book is important to use in your classroom every day, every week, or for particular paths of study. These units can be taught and integrated into any curriculum, such as Language Arts, Social Studies, Health, or Computer Sciences. There are lessons addressing specific curricular areas you teach during the year, and activities for issues that may arise unexpectedly. These lessons don't need to replace existing curricula but are designed to complement and enhance what you are teaching today.

How to Develop Parent and Community Awareness

New media literacy is not a job for teachers alone. It is a literacy that depends upon teachers, students, parents, the community, and the information and entertainment industries.

Students will be most receptive to this turn of events in your classroom. They may not believe that watching a movie or TV show is homework until they realize that analyzing, interpreting, and especially creating media are hard work and take deep thinking.

Some parents may be initially suspicious of this approach, as may be your community, but to prepare them to support you, share the Striking Facts sheet in English and Spanish (pp. 11–12) for starters. Bring it to "Meet–the–Teacher" night, PTA meetings, and parent conferences. If your school is able, send it, fax it, or *e-mail* it–the key is: Get the word out. Many parents think they should know how to understand today's media and explain it to their children, but most don't and have had no reason to know. This does not mean that they shouldn't. Parents need to know the extent to which media affects their lives, particularly the lives of their children, and that as parents, they control a good part of their children's media intake. Realize the extent of the media generation gap, and close it with the help of parents and your community.

With two thousand hours of television each day to choose from, it's not astonishing that parents don't know what to say to their kids about the prominence of explicit language, sexual innuendo, and overt violence. Provide the Just Think Guide (Appendix D, p. 173) for your community, or draw up a guide customized specifically for your parents. It will reinforce that you are connected to your students/their children, share the commitment and responsibility to your students/their children, and further support the relationship between home, school, and children, which is a lifeline that cannot be underestimated.

Please see the Next Steps section (p. 134) to discover how your students will be able to present their messages to parents, schools, and your community once they have participated in the Developing Minds curriculum.

The work of the Just Think Foundation agrees that young people may think a bit differently from generations before, but their insight and ability to understand through media is keener than ever. Young people don't just love media, their world experiences have grown dependent on them. When interviewed about their relationships with television, young people's comments ranged from "TV is my best friend" to "TV is part of the family."[9] One out of every four children offered $10,000 in exchange for their TV said they'd prefer their television.[10] This is possibly very different from the relationship you have with TV and is important to understand.

Find out if your parents or community members have complementary expertise or resources to contribute to the media messages your students will create. If any of your parents have dabbled in the media industry, they might volunteer time or equipment to supplement your program. Newspapers, magazines, taped TV programs, or CD–ROMs that students bring or loan to the class are great. When parents know what you are looking for, they can encourage their children to do the basic follow–through and bring additional resources into the classroom.

Stimulating critical thinking skills about the power of media in your classroom or school will allow you to quench your students' thirst for media without letting them drown. Teach them to use media selectively.

You will simultaneously help them discover and create new worlds with media, while refining their ability to work in groups and individually, strengthening study skills and computer skills, and preparing your students to foresee the great expectations their future will bring.

"99% of American households have televisions (more than telephones at 97%) and 57% of children in the United States have a TV in their bedroom."[11]

BASIC STEPS

How to Use This Book

"My message to the children of the world would be to communicate, understand, and get along. When people have problems, it's usually from not communicating well. If we learn how to communicate well when we are children and work things out, then when we grow up we can work toward living together in peace. We could use computers with interpreter software to talk to kids in all different languages all over the world to spread the word."

Andrew, 8
Tomball, Texas

Overview

This book is for fourth through eighth graders, but can be easily adapted to high school–age students. The more mature your students are, the more sophisticated analysis you can expect from them. Similarly, the media messages they conceive, and projects they produce, will coincide with their relationship to *media*. What is different about this book is its hands–on approach to teaching the theory and concepts of *new media literacy* through the creation of media projects. Your students will better understand media by constructing their own media messages.

This book can be used many ways. The introductory units in Step 1 are designed to be used consecutively as they spiral from one idea to the next, developing the analytical basis from which to proceed. Activities in Step 2, the issue–based units, can be integrated into the introductory units into subjects currently being studied, or as stand–alone units of study. They provide more opportunities for you to make connections to your students' everyday lives while fulfilling the requirements of most academic areas (see Curriculum Matrix, p. 10).

Throughout this book you'll notice many cross-references. These are designed for you to use like *hypertext* on the *Internet*. You won't be able to click and arrive; however, just turn the pages to link to related information or ideas. For instance, take a minute now to flip to the Curriculum Matrix (p. 10). The Matrix is designed to help you integrate the skills and content areas in this workbook into subjects you may already be teaching. Media literacy isn't a subject unto itself; application to issues and subject areas is essential. We also encourage you to link from italicized text to the glossary in the back of the book. Become familiar with terms you and your students will need to know. If you have Internet access, take time to explore the electronic reference tools in the resource area and compare them to, or use them in conjunction with, other print resources.

This book is designed using icons to assist you in finding the best way to create a path for teaching that is tailored to your instructional goals and the needs of your students.

Before beginning this course, we recommend a pre-test (pp. 18–25) designed simply to serve as a general gauge of your students' knowledge, understanding, and awareness of media and its effects. This should be done prior to the course, without any preparation. To assess your students' true media diets, have them complete the Media Survey, an important tool that asks your students questions about what they read, what they watch, and what they play (see pp. 14–17).

Their responses to the media survey will weigh heavily in maximizing the purpose of this program. The more you are able to integrate the media your students know and love, the more interested and involved they will be in developing skills to deeply reflect upon, *analyze*, interpret, understand, and produce media. If possible, administer this *survey* before you begin the course. Tally the results of your class's media preferences and use a bit of that information in each class you teach. You will endear yourself to students with whom you may not have previously found a connection when they find out you recall that they like a particular comic strip, magazine, or musical artist.

Additionally, Daniel Goleman's *Emotional Intelligence* is rich with studies supporting the importance of identifying the "other" IQ skills.[1] Many young people have not received encouragement to explore their thoughts and feelings, let alone express them clearly. Take a moment and ask your students what they're thinking and how they're feeling. This is essential because the literacy skills you are nurturing depend upon an understanding of how media can maneuver the heart and mind. This will become even more apparent when your students begin participating in the deconstruction and reconstruction of media messages, and conspicuously meaningful when your students create their own message from scratch.

Encourage your students to bring in their own media resources to *deconstruct* and analyze in class. Not only will this empower them as more active participants in the course but will take some of the logistical work of gathering media off your hands.

The units may be controversial for some parents. For this reason we have included a sample letter that could be sent home for parents alerting them to the topics that will be covered in your media literacy units (see Parental Permission Form, p. 13). You may want to customize the letter with your school name or district's letterhead.

Make it clear from the first class that the goal of this course is to impart the skills necessary for your students to create their own media *messages. Brainstorming, storyboarding,* and *constructing* posters, bumper stickers, videos, and *CD-ROMs* are terrific projects in which you can set inspirational expectations. No matter what the age group you work with, your expectations can be set quite high. Through the assessment of your students' final projects, their learning experience and comprehension will be evident.

See Next Steps (p. 134) to find ways to extend your classroom experiences into the *community*. There are numerous ways to link and extend what young people learn through Developing Minds. Peer teaching, student presentations to parents and the community, and teachers teaching teachers are some of the ideas suggested in this book and in the extensions available through Just Think's *website*, www.justthink.org, and other online resources.

Following Next Steps, there is a refined resource list of books, magazines, newsletters, videotapes, movies, CD–ROMs, and online sites that will exponentially augment the dynamic of your class. Because resources change rapidly, this is only a partial list.

To help stay abreast with new resources, please note the phone number and website address of the Just Think Foundation on the back cover of this book.

Copyright issues are important. Following are a number of resources to support your use of media materials while respecting copyright laws. *Cable television* offers 540 hours of *commercial*-free educational programming each month. *Cable in the Classroom Magazine* publishes the specific copyright restrictions for each program, many of which have extended clearance or unrestricted use policies; telephone: (800) 743–5355. *Copyright's Highway: A Tour of Intellectual Property Rights in the Electronic Age*, Paul Golstein, Professor of Law, Stanford University; telephone: (800) 786–3738. Educational use and copyright information website: www.copyright.com. Copyright laws change regularly, so check before you assume you have free use.

"Curriculum Matrix"

	Introductory Units	Issue Units	Media Projects
English-Language Arts:			
▸ Listening	X	X	X
▸ Speaking	X	X	X
▸ Reading	X	X	X
▸ Writing	X	X	X
Critical Thinking:			
▸ Describing, defining, choosing	X	X	X
▸ Interpreting, comparing	X	X	X
▸ Identifying, selecting, explaining	X	X	X
▸ Synthesizing through telling, creating, making	X	X	X
▸ Evaluating, judging	X	X	X
Health:			
▸ Respect for and promotion of health		X	
▸ Personal responsibility	X	X	X
▸ Informed use of health information, products, and services		X	
History-Social Science:			
▸ Civic values	X	X	X
▸ Constitutional heritage		X	
▸ Cultural literacy		X	
▸ Economic literacy		X	
▸ Historic literacy		X	
▸ Geographic literacy		X	
▸ Sociopolitcal literacy		X	X
Math:			
▸ Decision making	X	X	X
▸ Problem-solving		X	X
▸ Interpreting and graphing statistics		X	X
Multicultural:			
▸ Diversity	X	X	X
▸ Representation		X	
Science:			
▸ Classify and categorize	X	X	
▸ Studay relationship between conditions and outcomes		X	X
Visual & Performing Arts:			
▸ Aesthetic valuing		X	X
▸ Artistic perception		X	X
▸ Creative expression	X	X	X
▸ Historical and cultural context		X	X

"Striking Facts"

 "In 1950, only 10% of American families had a television set in their homes. By the end of the decade, that percentage had skyrocketed to 90%. Today 99% of American homes have a television set. More families own a television than a telephone. The average American Family owns 2.4 sets. Many children in the United States have a television set in their own bedroom" (American Medical Association [AMA], 1996).

 "Children now spend more time learning about life through media than in any other manner. Electronic media are prominent teachers of today's youth as well as being powerfully attractive to them. The combination of visual with auditory input makes television, videos, and video games much more attractive than other media such as books" (AMA, 1996).

 "The average American child spends approximately 28 hours a week watching television. In a year's time, American school children spend twice as much time watching television as they spend in the classroom" (AMA, 1996).

 "The amount of time spent in front of a television or video screen is the single biggest chunk of time in the waking life of an American child" (AMA, 1996).

 "In recent years the top selling video games have been Mortal Kombat, Mortal Kombat II and Doom. Each has been increasingly violent. The object of each is not to just kill your opponent, but to master the skills to do it in more vicious ways" (AMA, 1996).

 "Children's TV shows contain about 26 violent acts each hour. During an average prime-time hour there are five violent acts. MTV has at least one occurrence of violence in more than 50% of its videos. The average adolescent is exposed to some 14,000 sex-related references per year" (AMA, 1996).

 "Content analysis of television reveals that the average American child will witness 8,000 murders on TV by the time he or she is 12. They will see 20,000 commercials a year, and have viewed over 200,000 acts of violence on television, including 16,000 murders, before he or she turns 18 years old" (AMA, 1996).

For more information, please visit the Just Think Foundation website at
www.justthink.org.

"Hechos Que Nos Afectan"

 "En 1950, solamente un 10% de las familias Estadounidenses tenian televisión en sus casas. Al finalizar la década, ese porcentage ascendió a un 90%. Hoy en día un 99% de los hogares Estadounidenses tiene una televisión. Mas familias poseen una televisión antes que un teléfono. El promedio de las familias Estadounidenses posee 2.4 televisiones. Muchos niños en los Estados Unidos tienen una televisión en su habitación" (American Medical Association, 1996).

 "Los niños emplean más tiempo aprendiendo sobre la vida a través de los medios de comunicación que a través de cualquier otra manera. Medios de comunicación electrónicos son una prominente fuente de aprendizaje para los niños de hoy en día al igual que un fuerte atractivo. La combinación de imagen y sonido hace que la televisión sea mucho más atractiva que otros medios de comunicación como los libros" (American Medical Association, 1996).

 "El niño Estadounidense promedio pasa aproximadamente 28 horas por semana viendo televisión. En el período de un año, los estudiantes Estadounidenses emplean el doble de tiempo viendo televisión de lo que estan en el colegio"(American Medical Association, 1996).

 "El niño Estadounidense pasa la mayor cantidad de tiempo de su vida viendo televisión" (American Medical Association, 1996).

 "Recientemente los videos que más se han vendido en Estados Unidos son Mortal Kombat, Mortal Kombat II y Doom. El índice de violencia es cada vez más prevalente. El objetivo de cada video no es solamente matar al oponente, sino también convertirse en un profesional matando" (American Medical Association, 1996).

 "La televisión dirigida a niños contiene alrededor de 26 actos violentos cada hora. Programas de televisión que cuentan con una alta audiencia contienen un promedio de cinco actos violentos. MTV por lo menos tiene un acto violento en más del 50% de sus videos. El adolescente promedio está expuesto a unas 14.000 referencias sexuales al año"(American Medical Association, 1996).

 "Un estudio sobre el contenido en la televisión revela que el niño Estadounidense promedio al llegar a sus 12 años será testigo de 8,000 asesinatos en TV. Antes de llegar a sus 18 años, habra visto 20,000 anuncios al año, y más de 200,000 actos violentos, incluyendo 16,000 asesinatos"(American Medical Association, 1996).

Para más información, por favor visite el website de la Fundacion Just Think:
www.justthink.org.

Parental Permission Form

Name_____ **Date**_____

Dear Parents,

Our class will be starting a unit on _____ as part of our study of media literacy. Media literacy is the application of critical thinking to the messages of the media and is designed to help your child analyze, question, interpret, and evaluate the many messages he/she is confronted with every day. We are all concerned about the range of messages that are sent by the print and electronic media. Media literacy includes the skills and knowledge young people need to examine the wide variety of messages, to think critically about the content, form, and purpose of those messages, and ultimately become more discerning in their own selection process.

Due to the content of some of the lessons in this unit, I wanted you to be aware of the possibility of discussions that deal with sensitive issues, such as _____. We will be watching _____. The dates for this unit are _____.

You are welcome to visit the class anytime during this unit of study. I encourage daily discussions between you and your child to reinforce the goals of this media literacy unit.

Please feel free to call me with any questions you might have. In addition, please sign this consent form to acknowledge that you have read this letter and are aware of this topic we will be studying.

Sincerely,

_____

– –

Date _____

I am aware of the topic and the video clips you will be sharing in the media literacy unit.

_____

(Parent or Guardian signature)

Name_____ **Date**_____

Grade _____ **Gender** _____

"Media Survey"

Directions: Please read each question carefully, and take time to "just think" about your answers. For questions that ask "why," please write your answers in complete sentences.

1. List in order your four favorite media activities, and explain on the back what you like or don't like. (For example: reading/watching TV or movies/listening to music/using a computer, etc.)

    I. _____

    II._____

    III. _____

    IV. _____

Print

2. Name three of your favorite books or short stories and tell why they're favorites.

    I. _____

    II._____

    III. _____

3. Do you read just for pleasure? ☐ Yes ☐ No

4. How much time do you read each day? _____

5. Do you buy books? ☐ Yes ☐ No   How often? _____

6. Do you check books out of the library? ☐ Yes ☐ No   How often? _____

7. If you read, what are the titles of some of the books?

    _____

    _____

8. What is/are your favorite magazine/s? Explain why for each on the back.

_____

_____

9. Do you pay attention to the advertisements in magazines? ❐ Yes   ❐ No
   If yes, which do you look at in the magazine first? Advertisements? Articles?

_____

What ads have caught your attention? (Please name product or service advertising.) Why?

_____

_____

_____

10. Do you read the newspaper? ❐ Yes   ❐ No
Which one(s)?_____
How often? _____ What section(s)?_____

11. Do you read the newspaper comics? ❐ Yes   ❐ No   If yes, what is/are your favorite comic(s)?

_____

_____

12. Do you read comic books? ❐ Yes   ❐ No If yes, what is/are your favorite(s)? Explain why on the back.

_____

_____

Film/Movies

13. What is/are your favorite movie(s)? Explain why for each.

_____

_____

_____

14. How often do you go to the movies?

_____

15. How often do you rent videos?

_____

Music

16. What type(s) of music do you listen to?
❏ Rock & Roll ❏ Rap ❏ Pop ❏ R&B ❏ Country ❏ Alternative ❏ Classical ❏ Other

_____

17. What is/are your favorite singer(s) or musical group(s)?

_____

_____

18. When you listen to music do you care more about:
❏ The Lyrics ❏ The Way the Music Sounds ❏ Both

19. Do you watch music videos? ❏ Yes ❏ No
If yes, which is your favorite and why?

_____

_____

20. Do you prefer to listen to music or watch music videos? Explain why on the back.

_____

Television

21. What is/are your favorite television show(s)? Explain why for each on the back.

_____

_____

_____

22. Do you watch more TV before school, after school, on the weekends, or in the evening?

_____

23. Approximately how many hours do you watch TV each day?

_____

24. Do you pay attention to television commercials? ❏ Yes ❏ No
If yes, what is/are your favorite TV commercial(s)? Explain why for each on the back.

_____

_____

Video Games

25. Do you play video games? ☐ Yes ☐ No
    If yes, which is/are your favorite(s)? Explain why for each on the back.

    _____

    _____

Computers

26. Do you use a computer? ☐ Yes ☐ No   If so, what kind? _____

27. If you don't use one, do you have regular access to one? ☐ Yes ☐ No

28. Do you use a computer for: ☐ School Work   ☐ Recreational   ☐ Both

29. Do you use CD-ROMs? If so, what are your favorite CD-ROMs? Explain why for each on the back.

    _____

    _____

30 Do you browse the World Wide Web? If so, what are some of your favorite sites to visit?

    _____

    _____

31. Do you prefer accessing information using a computer or would you rather use books or other resources like the library?

    _____

32. Is there anything you'd like to tell us that we forgot to ask?

    _____

    _____

Congratulations, you've just participated in your first youth consultant focus group.
Once your teacher is finished working with your responses, please have him or her mail or fax them to:

Just Think Foundation
39 Mesa, Suite 106
The Presidio
San Francisco, CA 94129   www.justthink.org (website)
Telephone: (415) 561-2900   think@justthink.org (e-mail)
Fax: (415) 561-2901   justthink@aol.com (e-mail)

If you would like to be added to our online mailing list, all you or your teacher has to do is send a message to think@justthink.org and we'll add you as soon as possible.

"Pre-test/Post-test 1"

All of the following statements are false. When administering this test either in writing or orally, count the total number of students who believe these are true statements during the pre-test and post-test. These tests are meant to assess changes in attitudes and beliefs about the media.

1. Mass media are ways of presenting images and messages to a few people at a time.
   ❏ True   ❏ False   Explain your answer:

   _____

   _____

2. Media messages do not require close examination because they are easy to understand.
   ❏ True   ❏ False   Explain your answer:

   _____

   _____

3. New media literacy is the ability to write scripts for TV.   ❏ True   ❏ False   Explain your answer:

   _____

   _____

4. Society is a group of people who do things together in the evenings and on weekends.
   ❏ True   ❏ False   Explain your answer:

   _____

   _____

5. Newspapers, magazines, TV, and radio deliver news and information in the same ways in a democracy as they do in other countries. ❏ True   ❏ False   Explain your answer:

   _____

   _____

6. Population subsets on TV (such as the elderly, the handicapped, and teenagers) are always fairly represented. ❏ True   ❏ False   Explain your answer:

   _____

   _____

7. The physical human bodies shown in TV sitcoms and ads are usually realistic.
   ❒ True   ❒ False   Explain your answer:

   _____

   _____

8. Toy and game commercials on TV are always meant for both boys and girls.
   ❒ True   ❒ False   Explain your answer:

   _____

   _____

9. Each magazine ad is designed to cause similar reactions from all readers. ❒ True   ❒ False
   Explain your answer:

   _____

   _____

10. Violence in music, TV programs, video games, and movies has not been shown to cause social
    problems. ❒ True   ❒ False   Explain your answer:

    _____

    _____

11. Extreme violence is seldom shown in TV news reports. ❒ True   ❒ False   Explain your answer:

    _____

    _____

12. Tobacco ads are required to be accurate. ❒ True   ❒ False   Explain your answer:

    _____

    _____

13. Health and social problems have not been linked to the use of alcoholic beverages.
    ❒ True   ❒ False   Explain your answer:

    _____

    _____

14. Music lyrics always encourage desirable health habits. ❒ True   ❒ False   Explain your answer:

    _____

    _____

15. A celebrity is a person who is considered a good role model for young people. ❏ True   ❏ False
Explain your answer:

_____

_____

16. Animals and fictional characters cannot be heroes because heroes are real people.
❏ True   ❏ False   Explain your answer:

_____

_____

17. A leader is a person who has a strong personality and a good education. ❏ True   ❏ False
Explain your answer:

_____

_____

18. The messages of the media are meant to entertain and do not actually influence people.
❏ True   ❏ False   Explain your answer:

_____

_____

19. Young people can understand media messages but aren't able to create them. ❏ True   ❏ False
Explain your answer:

_____

_____

20. Creators of media messages are only concerned with content, not with the audience.
❏ True   ❏ False   Explain your answer:

_____

_____

"Pre-test/Post-test 2"

Objectives

These are the learning objectives ("goals") listed in each unit of the book. By administering these as a pre-test/post-test for each lesson, teachers can accurately measure the learning that takes place.

Unit 1: What Is This Thing Called Media?

1. Distinguish between the terms media and mass media.

2. List types of media (traditional and new media) and name the media elements in each.

3. List the similarities and differences in traditional and new media.

4. What do *author/audience* and *point of view* mean?

Unit 2: What Is a Media Message?

1. Explain how the author(s) and intended audience(s) affect the content of the message.

2. What's the difference between fact and opinion?

3. Give an example of a positive message.

4. Evaluate how the different media elements can affect the appeal and the emotional impact of media messages.

Unit 3: What Is New Media Literacy?

1. Name at least two alternative activities other than involvement with the mass media.

2. Explain some possible consequences of a particular "media diet."

3. Define new media literacy.

4. Name at least two technical components and elements of media messages and explain how they influence the content and impact of the message.

5. Can media affect your feelings and attitudes? ❑ Yes ❑ No Can it affect actions? ❑ Yes ❑ No Explain how.

Unit 4: Thinking About Community, Society, and Democracy

1. Community:

   Define *community.*

   Describe some roles the media play in a community.

2. Society:

   Define *society.*

   Describe some roles the media play in a society.

3. Democracy:

   Define *democracy.*

   Describe some roles the media play in a democracy.

Unit 5: Thinking About the Power of Images

1. Have You Seen Me?

   List some categories of population subsets (elderly, handicapped, minority groups, etc.).

   Describe some stereotypes that are in print advertising messages and TV sitcoms.

2. The "Perfect" Look.

   Describe the typical male and female depicted in print and TV ads.

   List some health problems related to being unfit.

3. What's Normal?

   Define *cultural norms.*

   Describe some current cultural norms that are frequently depicted in the media.

4. Target Audiences.

   Define *niche marketing.*

   Describe some niche marketing strategies.

   Explain why the media target specific audiences.

Unit 6: Thinking About Behavior and Consequences

1. Violence in Television and Movies.

   List specific types of violence that are depicted in children's TV programs and cartoons.

   Describe the "approval factor" for violence when it is used by "good guys" or in a humorous context.

   List specific information or statistics related to the effects of televised violence on children.

2. Video and Online Game Violence.

   Define *violence*.

   Locate some examples of violence in specific video and online games.

3. Inappropriate Language.

   Define *inappropriate language*.

   Describe some inappropriate language used in popular entertainment.

4. Violence in News.

   List some examples of violence depicted in news reports.

   Compare and contrast the news coverage of a violent story in various print and electronic news sources.

Unit 7: Thinking About Health Issues

1. Tobacco Use as Portrayed by Media.

   Examine and analyze some tobacco advertisements.

   List some health problems linked to tobacco use.

2. Alcohol Use as Portrayed by Media.

   Examine and analyze some alcoholic beverage advertisements.

   List some health and social problems linked to the use of alcoholic beverages.

3. Drug Use as Portrayed by Media.

   Name and describe some illegal drugs.

   List some health and social problems linked to illegal drug use.

4. Looking at Health Through the Eyes of Media.

    Explain how the use of tobacco, alcohol, or illegal drugs can affect health, lifestyles, and/or relationships.

Unit 8: Thinking About Real People

1. What Is a Celebrity?

    Define *celebrity*.

    List some celebrities and describe the reasons for their celebrity status.

    Explain whether being a celebrity equals being a "good" person.

2. What Is a Hero?

    Define *hero*.

    List some heroes, real and fictitious, from past and present, and describe the reasons for their "hero" label.

3. What Is a Leader?

    Define *leader*.

    List some leaders, real and fictitious, from past and present, and describe the characteristics or personality traits that made them leaders.

"Pre-test/Post-test 3"

This is an open-ended style of pre-test/post-test meant to assess changes in students' specific knowledge and information before and after the media literacy lessons in Step 1.

1. What is meant by the word *media?*

   _____

   _____

   _____

   _____

2. What is a media *message?*

   _____

   _____

   _____

   _____

3. What is *new media literacy?*

   _____

   _____

   _____

   _____

STEP 1   Introductory Units

"I think that kids all over the world need to know that we are the future. We need to be responsible for our education and our attitudes towards each other. I think we need to learn to be accepting towards people of all religions, races, and sexes. I think there should be an international 'Save Our Future!' day when kids all over the world meet in their school auditoriums, cafeterias, and classrooms to openly discuss these and other topics involving our future. These meetings could be videotaped, copied, and distributed (and translated if necessary) so we can see what kids all over the world think about these issues."

Shontay, 15
Silver Spring, Maryland

Overview

Just as family, church, school, and *community* play a significant role in the development of an individual's personality, values, and aspirations, so do mass media shape and influence lives. To develop the ability to think about the many ways media color their perceptions and beliefs, students need to stop, look, and listen to recognize media as an integral part of their everyday lives.

The activities in the three introductory units in Step 1 are designed to be used sequentially. First, basic terms and concepts are introduced. Then students are challenged to move beyond recall to reasoning, which in-volves higher, more complex levels of thinking: analysis, application, synthesis, and evaluation. In this way, students build on what they know about media and gradually integrate new skills and information. The introductory activities involve students in:

▸ defining terms, such as *media, mass media,* and *media literacy.*
▸ comparing and contrasting different types of print and electronic media, and categorizing them as traditional or new media forms of communication.
▸ examining how *media elements,* such as words, images, sounds, and *interactivity,* are used to create media *messages.*
▸ defining and applying the concepts of *author/audience* and *point of view.*
▸ recognizing mass media communication as *constructed* messages.
▸ analyzing media messages as *fact, fiction, opinion,* and *positive* or *negative.*

▸ accessing media messages, changing the form or content, and inventing new messages.

▸ evaluating how technical components, such as color and lighting, affect the appeal and power of media messages.

▸ interpreting and judging emotional responses to media.

▸ evaluating and reflecting upon the choices and consequences of personal media habits.

The *new media* literacy process outlined in this workbook involves a combination of lecture, critical dialogue, and active learning activities. In order to facilitate the process, use questioning strategies (see Guiding Discussions, p. 33) and establish these guidelines with your students at the beginning of the program:

▸ Explain to students that the media literacy lessons will involve looking at and interacting with a variety of media, and that they will be asked to share their personal reactions and emotional responses. Stress the importance of students being able to express themselves without fear of ridicule. Have students help develop classroom guidelines so everyone will feel comfortable discussing differences of opinion (see the Shared Decision Making sidebar, p. 117).

▸ Advise students that, whenever possible, they will be expected to bring in print and electronic media resources they may have at home to use in classroom activities. Remind students that they will be responsible for selecting appropriate resources to share with their classmates. Always take time to prescreen the media students bring to class.

▸ Share the goals of the new media literacy lessons with parents, and obtain their permission prior to showing controversial issue-related media resources in your classroom (see Parental Permission Form, p. 13).

▸ Provide media folders at the beginning of the program. Inform students that it will be important to keep their work organized in folders, which will be part of their final assessment. Provide blank sheets of paper in the folders and encourage students to develop good study skills by taking notes as they watch or engage in using various media in class and at home.

▸ Let students know that they will be making a classroom media scrapbook. Advise them to continually be on the lookout for information about media-related news or trends in a variety of media sources, such as magazines, newspapers, and *Internet* sites, so they can make regular contributions to the scrapbook.

▸ Establish an understanding and expectation of positive behaviors to be followed throughout the new media literacy lessons and the final project (see Interpersonal Skills section, p. 113).

▸ Motivate students by letting them know that their final project will give them a chance to be media makers—they will create a media message about something important to them, which they can share with others.

The lessons in Step 1 build the foundation for the discussions and activities in Step 2, which uses a thematic framework to engage students in examining important and sometimes controversial issues. Integrate at least one of the issue–unit topics into the introductory lessons, as shown at the end of Units 2 and 3. You also may wish to integrate the issue–unit topics into other academic subjects currently being studied in your classroom (see Curriculum Matrix, p. 10). Together, the discussions and activities in Steps 1 and 2 prepare students to successfully accomplish Step 3, where they will work together to plan and produce their own media messages.

Each part of the process is designed to work together to help students develop cognitive patterns that will become the basis for ongoing reflective judgment about what they see, hear, and experience through media. As students become more aware of how their media experiences affect the way they make sense of the world, they will be able to make healthier, more informed choices about their media habits.

What Is This Thing Called Media?

"I would like to tell kids to read. You can learn a lot from reading 'Build Your Mind, One Book at a Time.' I would post my comic in public places, such as libraries or grocery stores. I would go online with my plan and advertise by making book covers and screen savers."

Susan, 15
Pitsburg, Ohio

Students must step back a few paces and become detectives or mini-sociologists in order to examine the variety of media around them. Print and electronic media are so integrated into the daily environment that students infrequently acknowledge their presence. They may unconsciously notice and react, but they rarely reflect on the effect of messages in magazines, newspapers, TV shows, video games, or the *Internet* unless encouraged to "just think" about it.

In this first lesson, students begin working with the terms *media* and *mass media*. They identify what they already know by classifying many different types of media, distinguishing traditional from new media forms, and *deconstructing* the media elements (words, images, etc.) in each. They begin to look at media with new eyes–to recognize that mass media are "created" by one or more people and designed consciously for specific *audiences*.

Reproducibles
"Media Survey" (p. 14)
"Guiding Discussions"
(p. 33)
"How Many Can You
Think Of?" (p. 34)
"Whose Point of View?"
(p. 35)
"What Did You See?"
(p. 37)

Equipment
TV and VCR
Computer, video game
players (if available)

Purpose
Identify and examine the variety of *mass media* encountered in students' everyday lives and begin to *analyze* form and content.

Goals
- Define the terms *media, mass media, new media, multimedia,* and *interactive.*
- Identify various types of media and deconstruct their media elements.
- Compare and contrast traditional and new media forms of communication.
- Interpret the concepts of *author*/audience and point of view.
- Deconstruct the form and content of media examples.

Teacher Preparation

1. Provide a *new media literacy* folder for each student.
2. Copy the "How Many Can You Think Of?" chart on butcher paper—or write it on the chalkboard. Photocopy the worksheets.
3. Provide a wide selection of newspapers, tabloids, magazines, and other print materials (include liberal and conservative examples). If a computer is available, include electronic resources, such as *CD-ROMs*, video games, and the Internet.
4. Videotape either three TV *commercials* or three TV public service announcements (PSAs). Select examples that use different media elements, such as:
   - black-and-white images or text
   - colorful images with music (*special effects* or *sound effects*)
   - images with narration

Activities

1. Have students develop their own definitions of the following terms, then look up the definitions in print or electronic resources: *media, mass media, new media, multimedia,* and *interactive media;* compare their definitions with the ones in the glossary and come to a consensus.
   - Discuss the differences in these terms so students will use each correctly.
2. Distribute the "How Many Can You Think Of?" worksheet. Show students how to complete the chart by enlarging it on butcher paper or on the chalkboard so all can follow along.
   - Write in examples of two media types: one traditional, such as newspapers or TV; one new media, such as video games or CD-ROMs. Leave the Group, Author, and Audience columns blank.
   - Check off several media elements (words, images, etc.) in the example of new media; ask students to identify other traditional forms that could be considered multimedia, such as movies.
   - Ask students to give you examples of interactivity and explain how it's different from watching TV or movies. If electronic resources are available, have students use them to demonstrate the differences.
3. Students take their "How Many Can You Think Of?" worksheets with them as they break into small groups.
   - Give each group two minutes to write down as many types of media as they can (such as newspaper comic strips, TV *sitcoms,* magazines, video games, etc.), and fill out the information for each type.
   - Each group takes turns orally sharing items on their lists while you record their responses on the chalkboard or butcher paper.
   - Have students discuss why each group did not list the exact same examples.
   - Allow students as much time as they need to *brainstorm* other types of media not yet listed (cereal boxes, billboards, display ads, refrigerator magnets, etc.).
   - Continue recording until there is a long list.
   - Ask students to estimate how many hours each day they encounter the various types of media.

4. Have students develop their own definitions of the concepts of *author* (creator/ producer) and *audience* (viewer/consumer), then look up definitions in print and electronic resources; compare their definitions with the ones in the glossary and come to a consensus.

   · Explain that sometimes a message is created just for oneself, such as when you draw a picture for your own pleasure. Other times, it's made to be shared by many people, such as information broadcast on the radio or published on the Internet.
   · Write on the chalkboard:

Group	Author (creator/producer)	Audience (viewer/consumer)
1.	One	Oneself
2.	One	Another
3.	One	Many
4.	Many	Many

   · Have students identify the appropriate group number for the various media types on the list. Record the numbers in the Group column (e.g., group 2 or 3 for *e-mail;* group 3 or 4 for books; group 4 for video games, etc.).
   · Ask students if the Group 3 and 4 items are mass media. Why?
   · Have students identify the various authors or creators of mass media, such as TV producer, photojournalist, and so forth. Record their responses in the Author column.
   · Have students identify possible mass media audiences. Record their responses in the Audience column.

5. Distribute the "Whose Point of View?" worksheet. Have students develop their own definition of *point of view (POV),* then look up definitions in print and electronic resources; compare their definitions with the ones in the glossary and come to a consensus.

   · Have students record both the dictionary definition and the definition they developed on the worksheet.
   · Ask if each of the authors (creators) of media in their previous lists might have a different POV. Have students give examples.
   · Ask students to complete the rest of the "Whose Point of View?" worksheet as a homework assignment, due at the beginning of the next class.

6. Explain how to distinguish an *editorial* from a news story.
   · Have students locate, read, and discuss numerous editorials from various newspapers, magazines, or electronic resources available in the classroom.

7. Distribute the "What Did You See?" worksheet. Show the three videotaped TV clips.
   · After viewing all three segments, have students complete the worksheet.
   · Ask students which one of the three videos was their favorite (vote by a show of hands). Why?

· Have students compare and contrast the videos they liked best with the ones they liked least. What media elements were used? Did the selection of media elements affect their response to the video?

· Discuss changes they would make to the form or content of one of the TV commercials or PSAs to improve the message.

8. Pass out the Media Survey and ask students to complete it either in class or as a homework assignment.

Extensions

Have students:

▸ act out a historical event as a type of media presentation (radio drama, TV news program, etc.).

▸ create a media bulletin board for the school, library, or classroom, posting current information about the mass media, such as media-related comic strips or media-related news stories researched from a variety of traditional and new media sources.

▸ invite media industry representatives to a classroom panel to discuss the influence of the various media on our daily lives.

Name_____ Date_____

Unit 1
"Guiding Discussions"

Discussion and reflection are major strategies in the media literacy process. To lead a discussion that will solicit a response more thoughtful than "cool!," try the following questions to "scaffold" up to higher-level thinking.

Thinking about the media messages:
▸ What emotions do you feel?
▸ What do you wish was different?
▸ What are your personal reactions to ...
  · the opening or beginning
  · the plot
  · the background or setting
  · the music
  · the ending
  · the actors, people, or characters
  · the hairstyles, clothing, or costumes
▸ Was it believable?
▸ Was it realistic?
▸ Do you think the message will influence your opinions, attitudes, or actions?
▸ Why was this medium chosen?
▸ Is this message important to society?
▸ Can you recognize a recurring theme?

Thinking about the issues:
▸ How will this affect your life?
▸ What could you do to improve the situation?
▸ Has anything like this ever happened to you?
▸ What would your parents say about this?
▸ What would you change?
▸ How would this affect young children?
▸ What do you predict will happen in the future?
▸ Can you remember anything like this happening before?
▸ How is this different than it was one hundred years ago?
▸ Do you agree with the interpretations that have been offered?
▸ Can you give some supporting reasons for your point of view?

Name _____

Date _____

Unit 1
"How Many Can You Think Of?"

Media Elements

Author (creator)	Group	Media Types	Words	Images	Sounds/Music	Tradional Media (3 or more)	New Media (interactive)	Examples	Audiences

Name_____ **Date**_____

Unit 1
"Whose Point of View?"

Main idea:
The point of view can alter the content and the impact of a media message.

Dictionary time!
Write electronic and nonelectronic definitions of the term *point of view* here:

_____

_____

_____

_____

_____

What does that mean?
Write the definition in your own words:

_____

_____

_____

_____

Try these activities!
Select and cut out a political cartoon or comic strip and attach it to this page. Explain the point of view of the cartoonist:

_____

_____

_____

_____

36 ‹ Whose Point of View?

Read and cut out an editorial from a newspaper. Attach it to this paper. Explain the point of view of the writer:

_____

_____

_____

_____

Now, watch closely:
Watch a TV commercial.
What product was the commercial advertising?

_____

Explain the point of view of the author(s) or creator(s).

_____

_____

_____

_____

Okay, your turn!
Complete this sentence about the following slogans.

"Just Do It" means ...

_____

_____

_____

_____

"Just Think" means ...

_____

_____

_____

_____

Name_____ **Date**_____

Unit 1
"What Did You See?"

Please answer the following questions in complete sentences.

1. What was your favorite?

   _____

   _____

   _____

2. What stood out to you? (Was it certain characters or images or ... ?) Why did you remember it?

   _____

   _____

   _____

   _____

   _____

3. Was the message something positive or negative?

   _____

   _____

   _____

4. What would you change?

   _____

   _____

   _____

   _____

   _____

   _____

Referring to communication as *"messages"* helps personalize the concepts of *author/audience* and *POV*. Reinforcing these concepts makes it easier for students to realize that sometimes authors have personal opinions that influence the validity of their messages. This is fundamental to students understanding that what they see and hear in the various forms of *media* is not always the "truth."

The activities in this lesson give students practice in distinguishing *fact* from *fiction* and *opinion* and in differentiating between *positive* and *negative* messages. Through accessing various types of media messages and evaluating their personal reactions to them, students become aware that media affect their thoughts and feelings, and that some media messages carry more impact than others. This realization deepens as students apply critical thinking skills to exploring a specific media issue.

Reproducibles

PrintPaks Ad (p. 42)
"Mixed Messages"
(p. 43)
"Find the Message!"
(p. 44)
"What Is the Message?"
(p. 45)
Parental Permission
Form (p. 13)

Purpose

***Analyze* and *evaluate* factors that influence the content, form, and effect of media messages.**

Goals

▸ Apply the concepts of *author, audience,* and *point of view (POV)* to change the content of a message.
▸ Categorize and analyze media messages as fact, fiction, *opinion,* and positive or negative.
▸ Make a responsible judgment for selecting appropriate messages to share with classmates.
▸ Evaluate how different *media elements* affect the appeal and emotional impact of media messages.
▸ Improve the form or content of a media message.
▸ Examine and evaluate media messages about a specific topic; apply and share what they learn with others.

Equipment

TV and VCR
Radio with cassette or
CD player, laserdisc
player, computer,
CD-ROM player
Internet access
(if available)

Teacher Preparation

1. Photocopy the worksheets.
2. Collect and bring to class various types of print media, including newspapers; magazines; bumper stickers; T-shirts; books with words only and some with

photos, paintings, or drawings; posters; ads; cartoons; comic books; refrigerator magnets. Ask students to contribute to resources; be sure to screen each submittal for appropriate content.

3. If available, bring in additional media resources, such as cassettes or *CDs* with instrumental music, nature sounds or chanting; music or movie videos; laserdiscs; *CD-ROMs*.

4. Cut statements from "Mixed Messages" reproducible into strips, fold, and put strips into a box or bowl for a drawing.

5. Videotape several local and national newscasts containing *violence*.

6. Distribute Parental Permission Form.

Activities

If students completed the "Media Survey" as homework, ask them to turn in their *surveys*. Use this information as much as possible in selecting media resources for these lessons.

Remind students that they will be creating a media message for the class project, which is why they will need to take a closer look at how media are *constructed* to communicate messages.

1. Ask students to share and discuss their responses from the homework assignment, "Whose Point of View?"

2. Have students develop their own definitions of *message*, then look up definitions in print and electronic resources; compare their definitions with the one in the glossary and come to a consensus.

3. Distribute photocopies of the PrintPaks ad. Ask students to determine:
   · What is the message?
   · Who is the author? (discuss author's POV)
   · Who is the audience? (parents)
   ‣ Have students use their own point of view to rewrite the PrintPaks ad targeting kids as the intended audience.
   ‣ Share rewrites orally.
   ‣ Discuss how the message changed when written by a different author who has a different POV.

4. Discuss the definitions below. Give one example, then ask students to give examples of each of the following:

Fact: something that has actually happened or that has been proven to be true (discuss ways to recognize: observation, experience, research, etc.)

Fiction: something imagined, including characters, events, stories

Opinion: people's thoughts or feelings about what they believe to be true in their own mind (discuss belief, judgment, sentiment, persuasion)

Positive: a "yes" statement; favorable, supportive, trusting, or hopeful opinion or personal belief

Negative: a "no" statement; against, opposed to, distrusting, or unhopeful opinion or personal belief

▸ Distribute statements from the "Mixed Messages" reproducible by having students draw one message at a time from a box or bowl. Students take turns reading a message aloud, then discuss whether each message is:

    Fact, fiction, or opinion, or a mixed message?

▸ If mixed, which is a fact, which is opinion?

▸ If an opinion is stated, is it *positive* or *negative?*

5. Distribute "Find the Message!" and "What Is the Message?" and have students take the worksheets with them as they break into small groups. Form three or six groups, depending on available classroom resources (see following).

Three Groups (print resources only)

Group 1—newspaper or magazine headlines

Group 2—pictures or photos

Group 3—T-shirts or bumper stickers

Six Groups (print and electronic resources)

Group 1—newspaper or magazine headlines

Group 2—pictures or photos

Group 3—T-shirts or bumper stickers

Group 4—segment from cassette or CD

Group 5—clip from videos or laserdiscs

Group 6—segment from CD-ROM or the *Internet*

6. Students read the "Find the Message!" worksheet; find a message appropriate for sharing with the class from the media resources specified for their group.

▸ Students write the answers to the questions on the form about the message they found.

7. Ask students to take out the "What Is the Message?" worksheet. Remind them that they will be sharing opinions and feelings about the messages that others have found, and to follow the guidelines they developed about being honest and nonjudgmental.

▸ Beginning with Group 1, individuals in each group take turns sharing the media message they have found.

▸ After each message is presented, students use the "What Is the Message?" form to answer all the questions for that grouping (newspapers, pictures, etc.).

▸ Have students share and discuss their responses to all questions in each grouping.

▸ Repeat with Group 2, and so on.

8. Integrate activities from one of the chapters in Step 2: Issue-Oriented Units. Select a topic that relates to an academic area students are currently studying, to an issue that has come up in class.

During discussions, ask students to *deconstruct* the messages in the same ways they just practiced:

- · Is it *fact, fiction,* or *opinion ... positive* or *negative?*
- · Who's the *author?* Who's the *audience?*
- · What *media elements* were used? Which had the most powerful effect?
- ‣ How did the message affect them? What were their feelings and reactions?

Have students:

- ‣ view and discuss videotaped reports of violence from TV newscasts.
- ‣ discuss the unwritten motto of some TV newscasts, "If it bleeds, it leads."
- ‣ examine and discuss the images that accompany violent stories in newspapers, TV newscasts, and newsmagazines.

Extensions
Have students:

- ‣ write letters or *e-mail* to a local newspaper editor or TV news *director* expressing opinions about the coverage of violence in the news.
- ‣ collect the front page stories of a local newspaper for two weeks; analyze recurring themes; evaluate the reporting of violent news stories; share gatherings with students and parents at a PTA meeting or assembly.

"PrintPaks Ad"

Name_____ Date_____

Unit 2
"Mixed Messages"

Use all of the statements below, or select one or two in each category.
Key: F=fact; FN=fiction; O=opinion; P=positive; N=negative; X=none of the above

Be sure to trim key codes when cutting statements in strips to fold and place in a box or bowl for students to draw from. Have them read statements aloud, and state classifications.

O/P	Michael Jordan is the best basketaball player who ever lived.
F	A period is used at the end of a sentence.
O/N	One thing is clear, there's never enough snow in the winter.
F	If you put a penny in water it will sink.
FN	The mushrooms decided to go to war.
O	Bicycles have two wheels, so all bicycles should be designed for two people.
F	You can't always believe what you see on TV.
O/N	Girls don't do well in science classes.
O/N	Only boys do well in sports.
FN	The plastic horse began to gallop.
O/P	All babies are beautiful.
O/P	The best thing about measles is that they eventually go away.
F	There are four quarts in a gallon.
O/N*	Just say "no."
FN	When a cow laughs really hard, milk comes out of its nose.
X	All camels have three humps.
F/O	Gloves keep your hands warm. When it's cold, everyone should wear gloves.

*Negative statement used for positive purpose

Name_____   **Date**_____

Unit 2
"Find the Message!"

You know where to look ...
(magazines, videos, you name it)
for different kinds of media
(words, images, etc.—remember?). **So ...**

Look away and see what media messages you can find. Select a message you'd like to share with others.

It can be a positive or negative message, but if you select something negative, think about a positive solution.

START LOOKING
NOW!

Answer the questions in the space below or on the back of this sheet.

▸ What is the message?

▸ What media elements were used?

▸ Where did you find it?

▸ Who are the authors (creators)?

▸ Who is/are the audiences?

▸ Is this message: ☐ fact ☐ fiction ☐ opinion ☐ positive ☐ negative? How do you know?

▸ If you selected a negative message, how would you change it to create a positive message?

Name_____ Date_____

Unit 2
"What Is the Message?"

NEWSPAPER or MAGAZINE HEADLINES

Which one would you read first?

What do you think the story is about?

Do you think this story affects you personally?

Media: ❑ Words   ❑ Images   ❑ Sounds   ❑ Music   ❑ Interaction
Category: ❑ Fact   ❑ Fiction   ❑ Opinion   ❑ Positive   ❑ Negative

PICTURES or PHOTOS

Close your eyes. In the photo you liked best, what image or images stood out to you?

What is the thought or idea being expressed?

How did the picture affect you personally?

Media: ❑ Words   ❑ Images   ❑ Sounds   ❑ Music   ❑ Interaction
Category: ❑ Fact   ❑ Fiction   ❑ Opinion   ❑ Positive   ❑ Negative

T-SHIRTS or BUMPER STICKERS

Whick one was your favorite? What caught your eye? (words, images or?)

What is the message? (in your own words)

Does the message affect your life?

Media: ❑ Words   ❑ Images   ❑ Sounds   ❑ Music   ❑ Interaction
Category: ❑ Fact   ❑ Fiction   ❑ Opinion   ❑ Positive   ❑ Negative

CASSETTES or CDs

Which one did you like best? Why?

How did you feel while listening to it?

What were other times you felt like this in your life?

Media: ❏ Words   ❏ Images   ❏ Sounds   ❏ Music   ❏ Interaction
Category: ❏ Fact   ❏ Fiction   ❏ Opinion   ❏ Positive ❏ Negative

MUSIC or MOVIE VIDEOS or LASERDISCS

Which one stood out from the rest?

What would you change?

What is the message and how does it apply to your life?

Media: ❏ Words   ❏ Images   ❏ Sounds   ❏ Music   ❏ Interaction
Category: ❏ Fact   ❏ Fiction   ❏ Opinion   ❏ Positive ❏ Negative

CD-ROMs

What was your favorite? What was the message?

Which media element helped you most understand the message? (words, images, or?)

What's your personal reaction to the message?

Media: ❏ Words   ❏ Images   ❏ Sounds   ❏ Music   ❏ Interaction
Category: ❏ Fact   ❏ Fiction   ❏ Opinion   ❏ Positive ❏ Negative

What Is Media Literacy?

Media literacy, in its broadest sense, is the application of critical thinking to messages in the *media*. It is the combination of knowledge and skills required to access, *analyze*, interpret, and *evaluate* media messages to determine their purpose, composition, how they are conveyed, to whom they are relayed, and their potential impact. Students can then make decisions whether to ignore, imitate, or internalize the messages.

New media literacy means that this same combination of questioning and decision making takes place not only when students are reading a magazine or watching TV but also when they are engaged in playing a video game, exploring the *Internet*, or interacting with other new forms of media.

The following activities encourage students to analyze specific components that influence the effectiveness of media messages and evaluate how media messages affect emotions, attitudes, and behavior. Exploring these issues in the context of their personal media habits helps students apply new media literacy to their daily lives.

Reproducibles
"Create or Change the Message" (page 50)
"Analyze This!"
(page 51)
Parental Permission Form (page 13)

Equipment
TV and VCR
Computer, CD player, Internet access
(if available)

Purpose
Analyze and evaluate the impact of media in their daily lives and in the lives of others.

Goals
- Examine the choices and consequences of a personal "media diet."
- Define the term *media literacy*.
- Analyze technical components and elements of media messages that influence the messages' content and impact.
- Evaluate the effect of specific media on feelings, attitudes, and actions.

Teacher Preparation
1. Photocopy the worksheets. Make two copies of the "Analyze This!" worksheet (one for class and one for homework extension).
2. Videotape several TV *commercials*, *PSAs* and segments of *sitcoms* and news programs.

3. Videotape two or three children's TV cartoons with violent scenes and several scenes from children's TV programs, cartoons, and movies.
4. Collect a variety of ads from various electronic and/or nonelectronic resources.
5. Distribute Parental Permission Form.

Activities

1. Return "Media Survey" to students.
   - As a class, invite students to select one or two questions in one area (print, video games, etc.) from their Media Surveys to discuss.
   - Taking their *surveys* with them, have students break into small groups to share and discuss their personal preferences in those areas. Then have students tally the responses from members of their group.
   - As a class, tally the responses from the various groups. Compare and contrast student preferences. Draw conclusions.
2. Introduce the concept of a "media diet" and compare it to a food diet (individuals make choices and choices have consequences).
   - Discuss choices related to media (e.g., to agree or disagree, to watch or play with or not).
   - Have students list alternatives to being engaged with media (e.g., sports, hobbies).
   - Have students define the terms *passive* and *active*, then look up these terms in a print or electronic dictionary; discuss the consequences of passive versus active leisure-time activities.
   - Discuss what criteria, such as time of day, mood, or access, that students use to determine their media diet.
3. Have students work together as a class to create a definition of *media literacy* in their own words. Compare their definition with the one in the glossary and come to a consensus.
   - Outline and evaluate the reasons for learning new media literacy skills.
4. Show the videotaped TV *formats* (commercials, news, etc.). Ask students to take notes.
   - After viewing each video, have students complete the "Analyze This!" worksheet.
   - Ask students to identify which *media elements* and technical components relate to various media types (movies, print advertisements, etc.).
   - Have students evaluate the effectiveness of each technical component in the various examples. Ask them to explain how they relate and to give examples.
5. Have students evaluate how media messages can affect their feelings and actions.
   - In small groups, discuss specific examples of media messages that have caused specific feelings, such as patriotism, sadness, or fear; share at least one example from each small group with the class.
   - As a class, compare and contrast the type(s) of media elements, the message, etc. in their examples.
   - Ask students if they think feelings can affect actions. Have them give examples and discuss.

6. Show a TV cartoon that contains a violent scene. Have students name different emotions they felt while watching (e.g., happy, upset, disturbed). As you record their responses on the board, group together similar emotional responses.

   ▸ Have students select a color that symbolizes each group of emotions.

   ▸ Ask students to write down the color of their present emotion.

   ▸ Show other TV cartoons containing *violence*. Ask students to write down the color(s) of their emotions after viewing each one.

   ▸ Share and compare the various color(s) of the students' emotions before and after viewing.

   ▸ Have students create a *storyboard* for rewriting one of the violent scenes to make it nonviolent but still entertaining (see the Producing Media Messages section p. 115)

7. Integrate activities from Step 2: Issue-Oriented Units. Select a topic that relates to an academic area students are currently studying, an issue that has come up in class, or use the example from Violence in Television and Movies (p. 77).

Have students:

▸ view videotaped scenes from children's TV programs, cartoons, and movies that contain violence, and discuss why these programs include violent scenes.

▸ discuss whether other behavioral alternatives to violence, such as communication, mediation, or leaving the situation, should be substituted for or added to children's TV programming or movies.

▸ discuss the frequent lack of consequences for violent behavior portrayed in media, such as absence of injury, absence of pain, absence of repercussions for "good guys" or "bad guys."

   · what happens to the families of people who die?

   · what is the effect on the *community?*

Extensions
Have students:

▸ each select one media message from a print or electronic source to share with their parents. Together with parents, use the "Analyze This!" worksheet to record and discuss all of the media elements and technical components used to create the message.

▸ rewrite a violent scene resolving it in a nonviolent way.

▸ create a PSA to raise awareness about violent TV programs, cartoons, and movies.

▸ complete the "Create or Change the Message" worksheet as a homework assignment.

   · explain their choices: (1) find and bring in a media message that they have changed in either form or content, or both; or (2) make up their own media message and be prepared to explain what media elements they would use and how they would use them to communicate the message.

▸ To follow up the activities in this section with an issue-unit from Step 2 (pp. 53–105), select a related theme for this homework assignment. Or better yet, *brainstorm* the theme with your students.

Name_____   Date_____

Unit 3
"Create or Change the Message"

You know where to look
(you've done it before)

So this time ...

be prepared to show how you changed the message by

changing the content or

keeping the same content, but changing the format,

or organizing the content in a different layout.

(You get the idea!)

Or ...

create your own new original media message.

Select the medium or media to send the message, and

state how you would use the medium (or media).

This is your chance to show what you can do!

Take action—
Now!

Hang on to the resources and finished product to share with the class!

Name_____ **Date**_____

Unit 3
"Analyze This!"

Select one visual medium, such as a television commercial, a magazine article, a CD-ROM, or a music video. Write your choice here:

_____

Now use your investigative skills to analyze the various components that make up the whole picture or message.

Make notes here about the components as appropriate:

‣   actors selected for various roles

_____

_____

_____

‣   background music or sound effects

_____

_____

_____

‣   camera angles, lighting, costumes, makeup, props

_____

_____

_____

‣   script or text

_____

_____

_____

Continue your analysis by answering these questions:

    ▸ Was the presentation realistic?

_____

    ▸ Were the characters believable?

_____

    ▸ Whose point of view was represented?

_____

    ▸ Who was the intended audience?

_____

And now, your reaction:

Were you interested in the message? ❑ Yes   ❑ No

Why or why not?

_____

_____

_____

_____

_____

_____

How would you alter it to make it better?

_____

_____

_____

_____

STEP 2 — Issue-Oriented Units

"I would say ... get involved in all the issues that affect young people. Every day in the newspapers, television, and magazines we hear about things that are happening around the globe. At first glance, these things don't seem to affect us ... yet after a while, when we think about it, these things greatly affect us. Issues about politics, pollution, wildlife, and rainforests are major factors of our everyday lives. If we let politicians make laws or industrialists cut forests and trees today, then tomorrow these issues will be our problems. The main reason many people don't seem to care about what we think is because most of the time ... it seems that all kids think about is video games, toys, movies, and cartoons, but there are so many other things that we really care about. So let's start reading, watching the news, and paying attention to the media so we can form our views. Then when we know exactly how we feel, we can speak out and let everybody know that we care. Then hopefully we can really change things."

Amy, 14
Altoona, Alabama

Overview

In Step 1, students were introduced to the fundamental thinking that is necessary to question, *analyze*, interpret, and *evaluate messages* of the *media*. They've begun to investigate the creation, dissemination, and influence of media in their daily lives. The impact of these media messages can have long-lasting effects and can permeate all aspects of the lifestyle choices of young people. As Dr. David Considine stated, "In 1992, The Carnegie Council on Adolescent Development published 'Fateful Choices.' The study noted a plethora of problems confronting American teens including alcohol, tobacco and substance abuse, teen pregnancy, unsafe sex, fad diets and violence. The study also recommended *media literacy* as a necessary component of educational efforts to address these problems."[1]

In Step 2, the five units are organized around themes related to some of these and other ongoing social issues. These themes can be integrated into a variety of curriculum areas (see Curriculum Matrix, p. 10). They provide realistic exercises in decision making that can motivate young people to:

▸ look beyond self-interests to connect with *community* and *society,* and to analyze the roles media play, especially in the context of a *democracy.*

▸ recognize that media images have a tremendous impact on behavior, attitudes, and choices in life, and that critical thinking about the purpose of those images will help prevent being manipulated by them.

▸ question the quantity of *violence* in both entertainment and news media, and consider solutions and alternative leisure-time choices.

▸ acknowledge the impact the media can have on health and personal lifestyles, specifically focusing on tobacco, alcohol, and illegal drug use.

▸ seek out and identify appropriate role models and *leaders* who display *positive* characteristics and admirable personality traits.

You can select a single issue-unit or use as many of the units as appropriate to the curriculum and abilities and interests of your students.

The activities (discussions, research, reports, interviews, analyses, and personal reflections) that are embedded in these units will stimulate students to become active critical thinkers long after the lessons end. Each authentic task, such as writing a letter or *e-mail* to the creator or sponsor of a TV program, helps students recognize that they are truly vital members of the community–not merely future citizens. Journals, class scrapbooks, and reaction papers serve as outward evidence of learning and can be used as part of the assessment process. A personal journal will permit individual reflection without concerns about peer pressure or ridicule. To quote Marjorie C. Feinstein and Thomas L. Veenendall: "Using a daily or weekly journal for the semester provides the instructor with a complete picture of the student's understanding of the concepts presented and their application to 'real' life ... the instructor needs to emphasize the application of the concepts to experiences and not the experiences themselves."[2] The class scrapbook allows students the chance to collect and review a wide range of resources, research findings, and individual or group work. It also encourages parents, administrators, visitors, and community members to learn more about the topic being studied. Reaction papers are used to elicit higher-level thinking and personal interpretation rather than merely summarizing *facts.*

Although topics of the issue-units are interwoven with values, personal choices, and free-speech issues, they are relevant, dynamic, and essential because the subject areas are present in the lives of all children. The issues are drawn from students' everyday experiences, brought to life by their own creative projects, and provide a forum for exploration, discovery, and even resolution to issues that may be difficult to approach through traditional curricula.

Teaching about the purposes, strategies, and effects of media messages may, of course, open a "can of worms." One student may claim to have seen all of the latest ultraviolent movies, listing each one defiantly as a personal accomplishment. Another may proudly proclaim that the best programs are on cable TV, making students without access to cable TV feel deprived or resentful. Still another may cautiously reveal that his or her family doesn't own a TV or doesn't allow her or him to watch certain TV programs. Setting the class norms and the appropriate tone for class discussions is essential before and during the lessons. The class may divide into two camps: the "haves" and the "have nots" (referring to *cable TV, Internet* access, personal VCRs, etc.). This will discourage interaction and critical thinking. You can overcome this by using the classroom resources as the equalizer, so all students can contribute to the learning environment and be involved with the same experiences. Establish parameters, guidelines, and norms for both large- and small-group discussions. Listening, creating a meaningful dialogue, respecting each other's *opinions*, and developing an openness to new ideas are all part of these interactions.

To integrate the issue-units into various curriculum areas, teachers may want to team up. Merge curriculum areas, such as language arts and social studies, or work cooperatively with the school media specialist to achieve the stated goals. Each lesson in the issue-units includes opportunities for students to create media messages. The completion of one or more of these mini-projects will prepare the students to embark on their own long-term complex projects, as described in Step 3.

Media literacy is more than a series of skills; it is a process. Involving parents, family members, students from other classes, and community groups as the *audience* for student productions can stimulate fruitful discussions and raise community awareness. In addition, students are introduced to exciting career possibilities. Involvement with the local media is another desired outcome from these lessons.

Prepare yourself for some exciting discussions and debates on topics that can literally be the impetus for lifelong changes in attitudes and behaviors.

Thinking About Community, Society, and Democracy

"It's gonna be ours tomorrow, let's 'peace' it together today."

Randi, 13
Marlboro, New Jersey

The *community* in which we live has a significant influence on each of us. A true sense of community includes a bond that connects us to other people, whether it is to a local geographical community or to people with similar problems or interests. *Society* is a greater structure that allows people to have rules and procedures, a sense of safety and routine, and defined roles. *Democracy* is a style of government that encourages participation and free enterprise and includes a system of checks and balances created to prevent one person or group from becoming too powerful.

The purpose of the lessons in this issue–unit is to introduce these concepts and to facilitate student discussions about their own role in the community, society, and democracy. The intent of this unit is to enhance future learning, conversations, and career choices through students' understanding of how the *media* influence the public and play significant roles in a community, society, and democracy. The *interactive* lessons will help students realize that there is a bigger picture to examine–that the needs of individuals are indeed important, but so are the needs of the group, whether it is the class, town, or nation.

If you have access, use the *Internet* whenever possible. Access to the Internet gives students a new place to question, explore, and interact with information. It may be an environment in which they can more quickly find and better understand concepts that are sometimes difficult or obscure.

The study of community, society, and democracy is often relegated to high school curricula. However, a grasp of these concepts will give elementary and middle school students the necessary foundation to encourage personal involvement while developing the critical thinking skills necessary to *analyze* and reflect upon how the media shape individuals and society as a whole.

What Is a Community?

"I would tell all the children that they shouldn't live someone else's dreams or meet another's expectations. Children are the future of the world—they should have their own dreams and expectations and think for themselves. One day they can become something to help their future generations.

Since it would be impossible to tell every kid in person exactly how I felt, I would probably use any form of communication possible to reach all the children because they may not have access to some forms of technology. ... A collage of photographs and music are good choices because the others are sort of segregating against handicaps, languages and classes."

Amanda (age unknown)
Erlanger, Kentucky

Purpose
To develop an understanding of *community* and the role *media* play in communities.

Goals
▸ Define *community*.
▸ Examine the roles the media play in a community.

Teacher Preparation
Provide materials for a class scrapbook.

Activities
Have students:
▸ discuss the word *community*; consider different uses of this word, such as the "Hispanic community" and the "world community"; create a group definition and place it in the class scrapbook.
▸ list rules, common practices, and expectations for their own classroom community, including such things as who are the *leaders*, what is the purpose, what situations can change relationships, etc.
▸ make a composite list of specific instances where local newspapers, radio, and TV help to shape a community by reporting local news, giving information about upcoming community events, raising people's awareness about community issues, covering school or community happenings, etc.

Resources
Becoming an Active Citizen—kit (p. 139), *My America: Building a Democracy*—video series (p. 147) Cultural Reporter—software (p. 141)

57

▸ during a one-week period locate and bring to class some examples of the media helping the community, and place them in the class scrapbook with the heading "The Media Help Our Community."

▸ each write a response to the question, "If you could create a community of your own, what would it look like and who would be in it?"; share them with the class; place them in the class scrapbook.

▸ each interview a community leader, such as the mayor, city council representative, county commissioner, school board member, or a judge and uncover their ideas about how the media influence the community.

▸ invite the students' parents to an open house to show the scrapbook with communities the student designed; discuss the influence of the media on a community; have roundtable discussions focusing on the strengths and weaknesses of other communities where the parents have lived.

▸ each write a reaction paper responding to the statement, "The media shape the community."

Extensions
Have students:

▸ select a local newsletter or community paper and analyze the form, content, and *POV*.

▸ invite community members to a panel discussion to discuss "What Is a Community?"

▸ analyze newspaper *editorials* and letters to the editor that reflect *opinions* about a specific community issue, and then have each explain his or her stand on that issue.

▸ investigate how TV, radio, and print advertising affect local businesses and report the findings to the class.

▸ create a school or community newspaper; distribute it to students and community members.

What Is a Society?

"My message is to strive for the gift of world peace. I would print my message on a T-shirt and I would sell them worldwide using the Internet or America Online. With the profits, I would send the children of poorer countries free T-shirts, if they wanted one, but could not afford one."

Jesse, 11
Nazareth, Pennsylvania

Purpose
Help students develop an understanding of *society* and the role *media* play in a society.

Goals
▸ Define *society.*
▸ *Evaluate* the roles the media play in a society.

Teacher Preparation
Supply various reference materials such as electronic and/or nonelectronic encyclopedias, dictionaries, magazines, newspapers, and access to the *Internet,* if possible.

Activities
Have students:
▸ research the word *society* with small groups using various references such as electronic and/or nonelectronic encyclopedias, dictionaries, the Internet, and magazines, and then share the findings with the class.
▸ create a group definition for the word *society;* place it in the class scrapbook.
▸ in small groups research a past or present society, analyzing its type of government, *literacy* rates, economy, cultural norms, and the role of its media.
▸ discuss various social issues, such as homelessness, pollution, AIDS, drug use, or voter apathy.
▸ as a class select one societal issue; over a one-week time period collect articles from print sources and the Internet on this issue; read and discuss the articles to learn more about the issue.

- create posters that will stimulate direct involvement or solutions regarding the selected social issue, such as collecting canned food for a homeless shelter or giving out brochures explaining how and where to register to vote
- display the posters in busy pedestrian settings, such as the library, post office, or grocery store; gauge the success of the posters by measuring the actual response over a two-week period

▸ discuss the many roles the media play in a society.

▸ invite a person who represents a nonprofit organization (such as the Salvation Army, a center for disabled children, etc.) to visit the class for a discussion of important social issues and how newspapers, radio, and TV often determine which issues are "relevant."

▸ each select either a *positive* or *negative* role that the media play in society; do appropriate research; stage a debate on the various positive and negative roles of the media in society.

Extensions
Have students:

▸ each read a biography and give a *multimedia* presentation about someone who helped shape society or was a social activist (such as Cesar Chavez, Henry Ford, or Susan B. Anthony), and as a group discuss that person's influence on society.

▸ research a time period in U.S. history, and list the major communication changes (printing press, radio, TV, movie industry, Internet) in our society since that time period.

▸ write a short story predicting what our society might be like in twenty years, focusing on the roles the media will play, and how the students will deal with the expected changes.

What Is a Democracy?

"Treat everyone equally."

Efrain, 10
Costa Mesa, California

Purpose
Develop an understanding of *democracy* and the role *media* play in a democracy.

Goals
‣ Define *democracy*.
‣ Justify the role the *mass media* play in a democracy.

Teacher Preparation
1. Read aloud some stories that will help the students better understand the concept of a democracy, such as short biographies of those who helped shape our democracy (e.g., Martin Luther King or Harriet Tubman) or nonfiction books about the democratic system.
2. Supply butcher paper.

Activities
Have students:
‣ *brainstorm* answers to the question, "What is a democracy?"; list all ideas on butcher paper.
‣ attempt to develop a group consensus about the concept of democracy by using a democratic system; place the definition in the class scrapbook.
‣ *research* and *analyze* the role that newspapers and print flyers played before and during the U.S. Revolutionary War; share the findings with the class.
‣ research how news and information are disseminated in *societies* that are not democratic, such as in communist nations.
‣ analyze the role of newspapers, radio, TV, and the *Internet* in U.S. political campaigns.
‣ research the effects advertising has had on the U.S. presidential elections by using the Internet, magazine indices, or an encyclopedia (electronic and/or nonelectronic).
‣ predict the future role of the Internet in our democracy.

Reproducible
"Democracy Survey"
(p. 63)

Resources
My America: Building a Democracy, What Is a Democracy?—kit
(p. 152)
My America: Building a Democracy, Rights and Responsibilities—kit
(p. 149)
"Democracy in a Different Voice"—video
(p. 142)
The Democracy Project:
www.pbs.org/point/democracy/
Internet Public Library—Presidents of the United States:
www.ipl.org/ref/POTUS
The White House:
www.whitehouse.gov

▸ conduct the "Democracy Survey"; share the findings through a *multimedia* presentation.

▸ *brainstorm* ideas about a citizen's responsibilities in a democracy; incorporate ideas in the class scrapbook with the heading "Responsibilities of Citizens."

▸ work in small groups to create a poster, video, or multimedia presentation called, "What Is a Democracy?"; share it with a class of younger students.

Extensions

Have students:

▸ find examples of patriotic images, such as flags, apple pies, or red, white, and blue color schemes in billboards, TV *commercials,* or magazine ads, and explain the purpose and impact of these images (do they actually promote democracy?).

▸ invite a newspaper reporter or editor to the class to talk about how the media serve as *gatekeepers* in a democracy.

▸ contact a local radio *station* to determine the guidelines and an appropriate topic for a *PSA;* create a fifteen-second radio PSA on that topic; give it to the local radio station to use.

Name_____ **Date**_____

Unit 4
"Democracy Survey"

Interview five adults to complete the following survey:

1. Name one benefit of living in a democracy.
    _____

2. What would you dislike about living in a society that wasn't a democracy?
    _____

    _____

    What would you like about living in a society that wasn't a democracy?
    _____

    _____

3. In what ways are the mass media involved in the political process?
    _____

    _____

4. Complete this sentence: A democracy can only exist if ...
    _____

    _____

5. Name one responsibility an individual has in a democracy.
    _____

    _____

6. What responsibility do the media have in a democracy?
    _____

    _____

The Role
of Media

Purpose
Raise awareness of the influence that the *media* have on each of us.

Goals
- Create reliability standards for news and information sources.
- Interpret the influence that the media have on the *community* or the whole *society.*

Teacher Preparation
Collect different types of resources, including a TV program listing, phone book, encyclopedia (electronic and/or nonelectronic), newspapers, tabloid newspapers, magazines, and provide *Internet* access, if possible.

Activities
Have students:
- discuss and list the various sources of information that are available, such as TV, newspapers, radio, the Internet, etc.
- work in pairs, with each partnership choosing a slip of paper (cut from the "Scavenger Hunt" worksheet) and locating the requested information; share their findings with the class and talk about any problems or questions they had.
- question whether all sources of information are equally reliable, such as a tabloid newspaper versus a local newspaper.
- make a composite list of some criteria necessary to determine the reliability of a source, such as the exact *author* of the information or the date of the information; place the list in the class scrapbook.
- investigate how the media can influence public attitudes and *opinions,* and give specific examples of instances when media *messages* influenced them (perhaps to attend a movie, buy a product, or give to a charity).
- discuss the effect of instant media on the Internet (include topics such as changes in attention span, instantaneous messages, reliability questions).
- investigate who owns the media and who makes the selection decisions (such as what movies are made or what stories are covered on the TV news); what considerations impact their selection (business profits, etc.)?
  - evaluate their findings and predict what may happen in the future if only a few organizations own all of the news and entertainment outlets

64

▸ each investigate one media–related career choice, such as a newspaper reporter or *documentary* filmmaker, that could then impact the *community, society,* or our *democracy;* share their information with the class.
▸ create questions about the media's role in the community or society; invite representatives from local media organizations (such as radio, newspaper, TV, or advertising companies) to the class for a roundtable discussion on "How do the media influence the public?" to answer the students' questions; make an audiotape or a videotape of the discussion; place the tape in the class scrap-book.

Extensions
Have students:

▸ pose the question, "How do the media influence us?" in a discussion group on the Internet; follow and print out the resulting comments; share them with the class and discuss.
▸ start a student service club that will help the local community through the development of a specific media project (e.g., flyers promoting the local "Meals on Wheels" program, or a senior resources webpage).
▸ research and chart the ownership of some major media organizations, such as newspapers, TV and radio stations, TV and movie studios, and cable companies, by using the information from the Internet or magazine indices (see Appendix B, p. 155).
▸ predict the roles the media will play in the twenty-first century; create a *storyboard* for a future TV commercial that advertises a new communication or information device.

Name_____ **Date**_____

Unit 4
"Scavenger Hunt"

Cut the following phrases into strips; each pair of students should have one phrase.

▸ The time and channel for an upcoming movie on TV

▸ Yesterday's weather in Greenland and Fiji; compare the high temperatures for the day

▸ The phone number for a local pet store

▸ The names of the president's cabinet members

▸ The price of a used bicycle and the phone number of the person selling it

▸ The times on Saturday a specific movie is showing at a local movie theater

▸ The name of the longest river in the world

▸ A review of a popular music CD

▸ An ad for your favorite food

▸ The current best-selling fiction book in the United States

▸ The price of thirty seconds of air time on a local radio station

▸ The year that Babe Ruth retired from baseball

▸ The names of players in the NFL Hall of Fame

▸ The person pictured on the cover of this week's *Time* magazine

▸ The name of the president of the United States during World War I

▸ The main characters in the book *The Lion, the Witch and the Wardrobe* by C. S. Lewis

Thinking About the Power of Images

"Practically no one puts you down because of your shoe color ... so why do we put other people down because of their skin color?"

John, 11
Pittsford, New York

Young people are surrounded by images that speak volumes about specific products to buy as well as how to think, what to do, and who to be. The activities in this issue–unit will compel students to examine the images that bombard them and then stand back and reflect on the effect of those images.

In these lessons, students will collect print ads, research health issues, and create *media* presentations while they confront the various images that are part of the popular culture. Each student must decide to either imitate those images or strive for autonomy–decisions that have lifelong implications.

Through activities that encourage discussion, analysis, and evaluation, we can see personal growth and reflection in the classroom. For example, the cultural norms that speak so loudly to adolescents are listed, discussed, and *analyzed*, giving students the power to think critically about what is being presented and encourage them to be more discerning. The goal is for your students never again to be complacent about images in the media.

Have You
Seen Me?

Purpose
Help students identify and reflect on *stereotypes* in *media* images.

Goals
▸ List some categories of population subsets (elderly, handicapped, ethnic groups, etc.).
▸ Analyze the stereotypes that appear in print advertising *messages*, TV *sitcoms*, and on the *Internet*.

Teacher Preparation
1. Prior to this lesson conduct class meetings about the need to be sensitive to people who may appear or act different from their family members or friends.
2. Read aloud stories about young people who are handicapped or who represent a minority ethnic or religious group and the hardships they have overcome.

Activities
Have students:
▸ discuss population subsets and make a composite list of some population subsets, such as the elderly, ethnic groups, handicapped, social classes, women; place the list in the class scrapbook.
▸ over a one-week period locate images of young people who are approximately their own age in magazines, catalogs, and newspaper advertising; cut out the images; place them on a bulletin board.
   · discuss which students in the class are accurately represented in those images on the bulletin board and which ones are not
   · make a composite list of the population subsets, such as the elderly, ethnic groups, handicapped, women, etc., that are not represented in the displayed images; place the list in the class scrapbook
   · during a one-week period note print and online images of those subsets listed; *analyze* and *evaluate* their findings and draw conclusions about what subsets are represented most often in print images
▸ make a composite list of subsets that they believe are underrepresented or misrepresented in popular TV *sitcoms*.
▸ in small groups create three-minute scenes that depict people who are rarely or never portrayed in TV sitcoms or in a series on the *Internet;* perform the scenes for an *audience* and get their reactions.

Resources
I Will Sing Life,
edited stories by and
for children who are
physically challenged or
have terminal illnesses
(p. 181)

‣ each write a reaction paper about the stereotypes that are usually depicted in print ads, *CDs*, TV sitcoms, and dramas on the Internet.

Extensions
Have students:
‣ create a magazine ad for a well-known product depicting people who are underrepresented in print ads.
‣ each send a letter or an *e-mail* message to a member of a population subset (such as a blind person) who is rarely portrayed in ads or TV sitcoms, expressing *opinions* and concerns about stereotypes.
‣ each write a letter to the *producer* or screenwriter of a popular TV sitcom and suggest the addition of a character who will represent a rarely shown population subset.
‣ *brainstorm* ideas for a new comic book "superhero" character who is a member of a population subset rarely seen on TV or in the comic strips; select the best idea; submit it to a comic book publisher.

The "Perfect" Look

Purpose
Help students recognize the "perfect" physical attributes of many people portrayed in advertising and popular television programs.

Goals
▸ Compare and contrast the typical male and female images depicted in print, online, and TV ads to the average person at the mall or in their classroom.
▸ Identify and list some health problems related to not eating properly.

Teacher Preparation
1. Become familiar with the typical teen images in ads portraying males and females.
2. Videotape a popular "teen" TV *sitcom*.

Activities
Have students:

Equipment
TV and VCR
Internet access
(if available)

Resources
copies of popular
teen magazines
*Living in the Image
Culture*—kit (p. 146)
*Television: What's
Behind What You See*—
book (p. 151)
TV Guide magazine:
www.tvguide.com

▸ discuss the typical male and female images that are depicted in print or online ads.
▸ over a one-week period bring magazines, newspapers, and catalogs to class; in small groups create collages of male and female images from catalogs, magazines, newspaper ads, and online sites.
▸ identify physical traits depicted in the images and make a list of recurring traits.
▸ discuss whether the images are realistic and whether the students and their family members actually look like the people in the ads.
▸ invite a nutritionist or athletic trainer to the classroom (select your guest carefully) to discuss the requirements, restrictions, and long-term effects of being a model or bodybuilder.
▸ research the effects of eating disorders, such as anorexia and bulimia, in print sources like health books, encyclopedias (electronic and/or nonelectronic), etc., and the *Internet*; share the findings with the class.
▸ discuss various diets and other health issues related to eating.
▸ watch the "teen" TV sitcom together and analyze the characters' clothing, bodies, hair, makeup, etc. with regard to how *media* portray young people.
▸ discuss the "perfect" (i.e., unnatural) images often portrayed in the media and their direct and indirect messages to young people.

‣ note what the actors eat while on-screen, then write or e-mail a TV or film personality and find out what they eat in real life.

‣ each create a "Me" poster, with a drawing and text focusing on personal strengths, *positive* physical attributes, individual talents and interests; display the posters on the walls in the classroom.

Extensions

Have students:

‣ assemble a panel of teenagers to discuss how television, music videos, movies, and advertising shape self-concept.

‣ interview a healthcare professional to learn how to maintain the appropriate weight for their height, age, and gender.

‣ analyze the males and females that are shown in magazine ads from other countries; compare and contrast them to U.S. magazine images; share their conclusions with the class.

What's Normal?

Purpose

Help students identify current cultural norms that are portrayed in the media.

Goals

- Define *cultural norms.*
- *Evaluate* the impact of some current cultural norms that are frequently depicted in music videos, ads, or TV programs.

Teacher Preparation

Share with the students some fads of cultural norms that were popular when you were in school.

Activities

Have students:

- develop their own definition of *norms,* then look up definitions in print and electronic resources; compare their definitions with the one in the glossary and come to a consensus.
- make a composite list of toys that are considered "girl toys" (such as Barbie dolls and kitchen sets) and "boy toys" (such as guns and chemistry sets); discuss the list; place it in the class scrapbook.
- discuss why certain toys, games, and activities are meant for boys and others for girls.
- list some other activities or products that are "gender-specific," such as hair products, skin products, and shopping for girls; and video games, cars, and bodybuilding for boys.
- make a composite list of careers that have traditionally been considered "male" or "female"; discuss the reasons; place the list in the class scrapbook.
- identify some recent trends or fads that are popular, such as specific clothing styles or phrases, and discuss why and how they have "caught on."
- in small groups identify and list certain norms for young people and the reasons for their acceptance.
- list popular toys, movies, video games, or music groups and discuss reasons for their popularity.
- discuss how advertising, music, movies, TV programs, or the *Internet* play a role in defining cultural norms.

Resources

Magazines (p. 146)
"Open Your Mind"—
video (p. 148)
Girl in America—
video series (p. 144)

72

‣ each write a journal entry about the role the *mass media* play in determining cultural norms.

‣ design a mural (include the date) that depicts cultural norms that are currently popular; place the mural in the school hallway with a graffiti board for comments; analyze the mural and graffiti board comments.

‣ compare and contrast two current cultural norms.

Extensions
Have students:

‣ research popular TV *sitcoms* from the past five decades; explain how they reflected or created cultural norms.

‣ predict some possible norms for teenagers twenty-five years in the future.

‣ write an *editorial* about the importance of being an individual and thinking independently, instead of merely "following the crowd"; submit it to the school or local newspaper or school *website*.

‣ create a time capsule for a future class of students; place ads, photos, clothing, and other items that would help future students know what the cultural norms were at the time of the time capsule's creation.

Target Audiences

Purpose
Help students identify and *analyze* strategies for targeting specific *audiences.*

Goals
- Define *target audiences* and *marketing.*
- Evaluate why the *media* target specific *audiences.*
- Create ads for specific audiences.

Teacher Preparation
Videotape a variety of TV *commercials,* including some from children's programming.

Activities
Have students:
- look up *target audiences* and *marketing* in electronic or nonelectronic dictionaries and define them.
- research advertising and target audience using electronic and nonelectronic encyclopedias or the *Internet;* identify the largest target audiences.
- learn about Nielsen Media Research (*rating* system); research and investigate the reliability of their rating system; produce a report on the findings.
- during a one-week period listen to various radio *stations;* identify the most likely "target audience" for each one.
  - contact the radio stations and request target audience information about their listeners; request public information about their advertisers and advertising revenue
  - make a chart showing information gathered from each radio station; place the chart in the class scrapbook
- watch various TV commercials, including *Kidvid,* and speculate about who the target audience might be for each one.
- in small groups create print ads for nonexistent products aimed at very specific target audiences, such as eleven-year-old guitar players or owners of newborn puppies; share them with the class; display them in the school.
- invite someone from an advertising agency to visit, analyze the student ads, and discuss actual marketing strategies.

Resource
Selling Addiction—kit
(p. 150)

Equipment
TV and VCR

‣ list the various cable *networks,* such as *CNN* and Disney, and decide who their target audiences might be.

‣ discuss reasons why radio, TV, advertisers, and webpages target specific audiences.

‣ each select one print or electronic ad; analyze it to determine the most likely target audience; evaluate the ad's effectiveness to reach that audience; design a better ad to target the same audience.

Extensions
Have students:

‣ use the yellow pages to select one local company; contact it by phone, letter, or in person; determine its most effective advertising techniques and intended target audience; report the findings to the class.

‣ find columns, features, and ads in a newspaper that are aimed at specific subsets of the population rather than the general public; share them with the class.

‣ each create an idea for a toy that is designed for a small subset of children; describe how to best market it.

‣ go to a store or library and make a list of the names of specific magazines that are aimed at small groups of people, such as video game players, skateboarders, or skiers, rather than the general public.

Thinking About
Behavior and Consequences

In this unit, students will *analyze violence* in children's TV programming, movies, and video games. They will look at the way violent news stories are reported in various news *media*. In addition, they will examine the use of inappropriate language in entertainment media. All of these opportunities for critical thinking about violence and language in the media will help students develop personal standards.

The facilitator can guide discussions and activities without restricting individual thought. The goal is to always allow students to work their way through the activities and think critically about behavior and social consequences. Violence, whether physical or verbal, is a part of life and literature; to either legislate it out of existence or to give it a blanket endorsement prevents critical thinking and personal decision making. When students are knowledgeable and discerning, they will begin to *evaluate* the violence in both entertainment and news.

Communication with parents and administrators regarding the topics covered in this unit is essential. Invite *community*, family, staff, and principals to the class sessions to involve them in the *media literacy* process.

Encourage students to discuss the topics with their parents, and then continue the dialogue after the unit has ended.

Our *society* is struggling with issues related to the portrayal of violence in the entertainment and news media. Rarely do adults have open conversations with students about the escalating use of inappropriate language in music, movies, TV, print publications, and the *Internet*. The activities in this unit can be the catalyst for students to "just think" about real–life dilemmas facing our culture.

Violence in Television and Movies

"Children of the world, look and see ... all the violence around you and me. We are the future, tomorrow is our day ... let's stop the violence ... in any way. ..."

Robert, 13
Atlanta, Georgia

Purpose
Raise students' awareness about the extent of *violence* in children's programming.

Goals
▸ List specific types of violence that are depicted in children's TV programs, cartoons, and movies.
▸ Examine the quantity of violence in *media,* and the acceptance of violence, particularly when used by "good guys" or in a humorous context.
▸ Describe the effects of televised violence on children.

Teacher Preparation
1. Become familiar with current children's TV programs, cartoons, and movies that contain violence.
2. Videotape several scenes in cartoons, children's TV programs, or movies containing violence.

Reproducibles
"Student Television Interview" (p. 79)
"Television and Movie Violence Checklist" (p. 81)

Activities
Have students:
▸ create a group definition of the word *violence;* look up the word in an electronic or print dictionary; place the definition in the class scrapbook.
▸ view violent scenes from children's TV programs, cartoons, and movies, and then discuss why these programs include violent scenes.
▸ identify the use of humor in violent cartoon scenes.
▸ select a cartoon or children's program that has been cited as containing violence, such as *X–Men, Mighty Morphin Power Rangers,* or *Teenage Mutant Ninja Turtles,* and each watch an episode together with a child eight years old or younger (who has permission to watch it).

- complete the "Student Television Interview" form (pp. 79–80); compare the answers
- discuss possible reasons for differences in the answers
▸ discuss whether other behavioral alternatives to violence, like communication, mediation, or leaving the situation, should be substituted for or added to children's TV programming or movies.
▸ complete the "Television and Movie Violence Checklist" (p. 81) and compare answers.
- use the checklist each time they watch a movie and discuss the findings with friends or family members
▸ discuss some possible effects that may result from depicting violence as humorous.
▸ in small groups *evaluate* violence used by "good guys"; discuss whether this violence is acceptable or appropriate; share the ideas with the whole class.
▸ discuss the frequent lack of consequences for violent behavior portrayed in media, such as absence of injury, absence of pain, absence of repercussions for "good guys" or "bad guys."
- what happens to families of people who die?
- what is the effect on the *community*?
▸ make a list of favorite nonviolent movies and reasons why they are good movies; publish the list in a brochure for parents; place the list in the class scrapbook.
▸ create a group definition of the word *censorship;* look up the word in an electronic or print dictionary; place the definition in the class scrapbook.
- discuss whether violence is ever acceptable and under what circumstances should it be censored (ask students if they would let their little sister or brother watch a very violent program).
▸ develop a list of creative strategies for parents who are interested in limiting their children's exposure to violence on TV.
▸ *e-mail* or write a letter to a TV *station* that airs a violent children's program or cartoon where the violence is superfluous or gratuitous; suggest alternative ideas for children's programs and stress the importance of nonviolent programming.

Resources

Media Violence and Children: A Guide for Parents—brochure (p. 147)
Decisions, Decisions: Violence in the Media—software (p. 142)
Beyond Blame: Challenging Violence in the Media—kit (p. 139)
Act Against Violence Campaign: www.krma.org/aav/medialit.html
Just Think Foundation: www.justthink.org
WNET TV Station Peaceful Solutions: www.wnet.org/wnetschool/peaceful/index.html
Street Soldiers Solutions to Violence: www.street-soldiers.org

Equipment
TV and VCR
Computer, WebTV, Internet access (if available)

Extensions

Have students:
▸ create two composite lists: favorite movies that are considered violent and favorite movies that do not contain violence; compare and discuss the movies; decide whether the violence was necessary to communicate the story (was it realistic, was it necessary?).
▸ rewrite a violent scene in a program resolving it in a nonviolent way.
▸ create and conduct a *survey* to determine the most popular children's TV programs, cartoons, movies; list reasons why they are popular.
- watch the three most popular shows listed in the survey findings to determine whether these programs contain violence; draw conclusions about the findings
▸ create a *PSA* to raise awareness about violent television programs, cartoons, and movies.

Name_____   **Date**_____

Unit 6

"Student Television Interview"

A. Plan to watch a children's television program, cartoon, or movie that is said to be violent. Ask a child between the ages of six and eight who is allowed to watch the program to view it with you. Before the program begins, ask the child these questions, writing down or tape-recording the answers:

1. What does the word *violence* mean?

    _____

    _____

    _____

2. Name some examples of violent behavior.

    _____

    _____

    _____

3. Have you watched this program before? ❏ Yes ❏ No   Why/why not?

    _____

    _____

    _____

4. Do you enjoy watching this show? ❏ Yes ❏ No   Why/why not?

    _____

    _____

    _____

5. Have you ever seen real people act the way the main characters in this program often do?
    ❏ Yes ❏ No

B. Watch the selected program with the child, and then ask:

1. Was this program violent? ❑ Yes ❑ No   Explain your answer.

    _____

    _____

    _____

2. Name some examples of violent scenes or behavior you saw during the TV show.

    _____

    _____

3. Name examples of the "good guys" using violence.

    _____

    _____

    _____

4. What would happen in real life if someone did these things?

    _____

    _____

    _____

5. Did anyone seem to get hurt or die in this program? ❑ Yes ❑ No

    _____

    _____

    _____

6. Did some of the violence seem funny? ❑ Yes ❑ No   Why/why not?

    _____

    _____

    _____

Name_____ **Date**_____

Unit 6
"Television and Movie Violence Checklist"

Complete this checklist about the depiction of violence as you watch the selected movie.

Title of movie: _____

Specific conflicts that are shown: _____

_____

Weapons used: _____

_____

Total number of deaths (keep running tally here): _____

Total number of injuries (keep running tally here): _____

Violence that is depicted as humorous (list the scenes): _____

_____

_____

Consider the consequences of violence on either the victim(s) or the perpetrator(s). Consider short-term consequences, such as bleeding or being taken to the hospital, or long-term consequences, such as convalescing in a wheelchair or the economic impact on the family. _____

_____

Scenes where "bad guys" used violence:_____

_____

_____

Scenes where "good guys" used violence: _____

_____

Other concerns:_____

_____

_____

_____

_____

Inappropriate Language in Media Messages

Purpose

Raise student awareness about *inappropriate language* in popular entertainment *media.*

Goals

▸ Define *inappropriate language.*
▸ Identify the inappropriate language used in popular entertainment.
▸ Justify the reasons for appropriate language.

Teacher Preparation

1. Become familiar with inappropriate language (profanity, hate language, racial slurs, put-downs, etc.) that is frequently found in current movies, music videos, music lyrics, TV programs, and print materials.
2. Videotape segments of movies, music videos, or TV programs that contain inappropriate language.
3. Collect print materials that contain inappropriate language.

Equipment
TV and VCR

Activities

Have students:

▸ watch videotaped segments from movies, music videos, or TV programs that contain inappropriate language.
▸ create a group definition of inappropriate language to include profanity, hate language, racial slurs, and put-downs.
▸ make a list of movies, songs, or TV shows that contain inappropriate language.
▸ discuss possible reasons for the inappropriate language that is often found in entertainment.
▸ during a one-week period keep a log of instances of inappropriate language in entertainment; discuss the findings.
▸ answer this question in small groups: "Has someone's inappropriate language ever affected you?"
▸ rewrite a specific scene in a movie or TV program to replace the inappropriate language with appropriate language.
▸ each select and complete one of the following actions regarding inappropriate language:
  · write a letter to the editor of a local newspaper

- write an *editorial* for the school newspaper or the school's *home page*
- *e-mail* or write a letter to the creator or sponsor of a TV program that has included inappropriate language
- initiate a student dialogue about inappropriate language and its effects on individual self-esteem

▸ list specific ways that society can limit or discourage inappropriate language.

Extensions

Have students:

▸ create a *PSA* to raise awareness about the harmful effects of inappropriate language.

▸ begin a dialogue in an *Internet* chat room about the short-term and long-term effects of inappropriate language.

▸ organize a panel discussion inviting community members to discuss the importance of language in a civilized society.

▸ in small groups create a slogan or bumper sticker about the importance of language or the *negative* feelings generated by inappropriate language; reproduce and distribute them in the *community*.

Video and Online Game Violence

Purpose
Raise awareness about the amount of *violence* in video and online games.

Goals
▸ Define *violence.*
▸ Locate examples of violence in specific video and online games.
▸ Design an idea for a nonviolent video or online game.

Teacher Preparation
Become familiar with popular video and online games.

Activities
Have students:
▸ review the group definition for *violence.*
▸ discuss their favorite video and online games and reasons for their choices.
▸ speculate about possible reasons why video and online game makers incorporate violence in games.
▸ discuss some possible effects of violent video and online games on children.
▸ discuss the differences between real-life violence and television or film violence.
▸ work in small groups to create an idea for a nonviolent video or online game that would be exciting, *interactive,* and fun to play.
  · share and discuss the proposed game ideas with the entire class
▸ select one of the new game ideas for a class project.
  · design and draw scenes for the new game; place these in the class scrapbook
  · develop an advertising strategy for selling the nonviolent game
▸ create a poster, bulletin board, or webpage to share what they have learned about video and online game violence and the possible effects on children.

Resources
"Are Video Games
Too Violent?"
Zillions magazine,
April/May 1994
(p. 153)

Extensions
Have students:
▸ plan a "No Violent Video and Online Games" week during which students share and describe nonviolent video and online games.
▸ plan and conduct a panel discussion with local *community leaders* about violence in video and online games.
▸ develop a *storyboard* for the new nonviolent video or online game; send the idea and storyboard to a video or online game company.

Violence in the News

Purpose
Raise student awareness about the frequency of *violence* in news reports.

Goals
▸ List examples of violence depicted in news reports.
▸ Compare and contrast the news coverage of a violent story in various news sources.

Teacher Preparation
1. Become familiar with available news services, including local, regional, and national news reports via TV, newspapers, magazines, and the *Internet.*
2. Videotape several local and national newscasts containing violent scenes.
3. Obtain newspapers and age-appropriate newsmagazines (*Time for Kids, Vibe,* etc.).

Activities
Have students:
▸ define what would constitute "violence" in news stories.
▸ view and discuss videotaped reports of violence from TV newscasts.
▸ discuss the unwritten motto of some TV newscasts, "If it bleeds, it leads."
▸ watch the same local TV newscast for an entire week and keep daily notes on:
   · news teasers (brief headlines used to catch viewers' attention)
   · the lead story each day
   · the total number of stories that contain violence
   · the news story that receives the most airtime each day
   · the images chosen for the news stories that include violence
   · *construct* a chart with the information from the week's research
▸ compare and contrast the same violent news story as presented in various news sources (TV, radio, magazine, newspaper, online news services).
   · draw conclusions about the coverage of violence in various news sources
▸ examine and discuss the images that accompany violent stories in newspapers, TV newscasts, and newsmagazines.
▸ discuss the concept of "family-friendly" newscasts—those that are designed to show fewer violent and sensational visuals.
▸ discuss differences between viewing violence in the news and viewing violence in entertainment.

Resource
"Creating Critical TV Viewers"—kit (p. 141)

Equipment
TV and VCR
Computers, Internet access (if available)

▸ discuss the need to protect children involved in news stories versus the need to deliver all of the *facts* of a news story to the public.

▸ each write a reaction paper about a report of a violent news story; place them in the class scrapbook.

Extensions

Have students:

▸ write letters or *e-mail* to a local newspaper editor or TV news *director* expressing *opinions* about the coverage of violence in the news.

▸ collect the front page stories of a local newspaper for two weeks; analyze recurring themes; *evaluate* the reporting of violent news stories; share gatherings with students and parents at a PTA meeting or assembly.

▸ create a list of standards on how a local newspaper or local TV news program should deal with violent news stories, and send the list to the owner, news director, or editor.

Thinking About Health Issues

The long-term and subtle effects of alcohol and tobacco advertising on young people are alarming. Ask the typical ten year old what brand of cigarettes or beer that she/he would choose if old enough to smoke or drink, and the emphatic brand allegiance of the child might surprise you. Whether the advertisers intentionally target children and teenagers is no longer the issue. The *messages* impact the child's immature and unsophisticated mind, whether deliberately or not. The depiction of tobacco, alcohol, and illegal drug use in movies, ads, music, TV programs, and the *Internet* should not be ignored. Young people must be armed with more than *facts* about health; they also need to know about the economic implications for media makers.

There are enticing strategies used in advertising and the entertainment media that deliberately make tobacco and alcohol use seem pleasurable, exciting, and socially appropriate. By analyzing these techniques, students may be less likely to be manipulated.

The popular culture tells young people that "If it feels good, do it" at the very time they are struggling with personal ideas of independence and rules of the family, school, and *community*. Children can be coached to "read between the lines" and understand the motivations of the advertisers, *media* makers, and drug dealers.

Health decisions have lifelong implications, and the choices made by teenagers can determine the future course of their lives. The alcohol, tobacco, and drug abuse in our culture is too important to ignore. Lessons that cause students to learn facts about potential health dangers, study the attitudes of adults, examine recurring themes in alcohol and tobacco ads, focus on the myths and exaggerations in media presentations, and create new *positive* media messages can encourage critical thinking about these important topics.

Tobacco Use as Portrayed by Media

Purpose
Raise awareness about how tobacco use is portrayed in the *media* and the health issues related to tobacco use.

Goals
- *Analyze* some tobacco advertisements.
- Compare and contrast facts about health problems linked to tobacco use.

Teacher Preparation
Collect tobacco products print ads and mount each one on a sheet of construction paper.

Resources

Fronske Health Center
Health Education
Brochures:
www.nau.edu/
~fronske/broch.html
(p. 143)
"Smoke Alarm:
The Unfiltered Truth"—
(p. 150)

Activities
Have students:
- discuss reasons for the use of tobacco products by adults and teenagers.
- research health problems that have been linked to tobacco use; share the information with the class.
- discuss the purpose and *target audiences* of tobacco advertising.
- during a one-week period list all print tobacco ads they see, noting the location, images, *message,* and possible intended *audiences* of each one.
- in small groups examine the selected (mounted) magazine tobacco ads and discuss the color, font, layout, people pictured, intended audience, and implied message in each ad; discuss common themes, images, and messages in the magazine ads.
- create a bulletin board specifying the demographic groups that tobacco ads in magazines are targeting, such as ads aimed at young college men, specific minority groups, professional women, etc.
- compare and contrast the myths (such as "tobacco use will make you appear more sophisticated") with the facts about tobacco use.
- in small groups create some realistic tobacco ads that are accurate and descriptive; display the new ads in a heavily traveled area, such as a school hallway or cafeteria, a fast-food restaurant, or a movie theater; determine the impact of these ads by surveying those passing by; discuss the *survey* findings; place posters in the class scrapbook.
- develop and justify a new "no smoking" campaign for young people.

Extensions

Have students:

‣ investigate and discuss the total advertising budget spent by various tobacco companies in the United States and worldwide.

‣ create and conduct a survey of students to determine their attitudes about smoking or chewing tobacco products; tally the results; draw conclusions.

‣ during a two-week period note the frequency, situation, and users of tobacco products in movies, TV programs, and music videos, and speculate about why this behavior was shown.

‣ *analyze* tobacco product advertisements at sporting events, and express *opinions* in letters to sports teams or tobacco companies.

‣ investigate tobacco-related *websites* on the *Internet;* share findings with the class.

‣ research advertising campaigns and government regulations of tobacco product ads in other countries.

Alcohol Use as Portrayed by Media

Purpose
Raise awareness about how alcohol use is portrayed in the *media* and the health issues related to alcohol use.

Goals
- *Analyze* some alcoholic beverage advertisements.
- Describe some health and social problems linked to the use of alcoholic beverages.

Teacher Preparation
1. Collect alcoholic beverage print ads and mount each one on a sheet of construction paper.
2. Videotape several TV beer *commercials*.
3. Provide reference materials.

Activities
Have students:

Resources
Selling Addiction—kit
(p. 150)

Equipment
TV and VCR
Internet access
(if available)

- discuss possible reasons for the general acceptance of alcoholic beverages by adults and teenagers.
- in small groups list as many beer brands as possible in two minutes; compare findings; discuss how they knew so many brand names.
- discuss the purpose and intended *audiences* of alcoholic beverage advertising.
- research and report on specific health problems that have been linked directly (e.g., alcoholism) and indirectly (e.g., death or injury resulting from drunk drivers) to alcoholic beverage use.
- in small groups examine the selected (mounted) alcoholic beverage ads from magazines; discuss the purpose, content, and intended audience for each one.
- locate, examine, and discuss alcoholic beverage websites on the *Internet;* speculate about the intended audience for each one.
- locate and discuss specific references to alcoholic beverage use in music lyrics, music videos, and music magazines and *evaluate* the attitude regarding alcohol use in the references.
- during a two-week period document all alcoholic beverage use portrayed in movies, music videos, and TV programs; compare and contrast alcohol use in the various media; share the findings with the class.

‣ research the laws, regulations, and restrictions regarding alcoholic beverage use on TV and in the movies; compare these to any restrictions on alcohol beverage ads in magazines, newspapers, and commercial online sites.

‣ view TV beer commercials; list and discuss recurring themes; speculate about reasons for recurring themes.

‣ invite a social worker, police officer, lawyer, or judge to the classroom to discuss social and *community* problems related to the use of alcoholic beverages.

‣ develop a composite list comparing the real consequences of alcoholic beverage use with the portrayal of alcoholic beverage use in TV programs, music videos, and the movies; place it in the class scrapbook.

Extensions

Have students:

‣ create and tape a thirty-second TV or radio *PSA* in the form of a parody of an existing alcoholic beverage ad, portraying real dangers related to alcoholic beverage use.

‣ discuss with their parents the "social" use of alcoholic beverages.

‣ in small groups write lyrics and music for an original song that warns young people about alcohol use and misleading alcoholic beverage advertising *messages;* select the best one; create a music video for the new song; invite parents to a evening session and perform the music video; share the findings of the class investigations.

Drug Use as Portrayed by Media

"If there was a message I could send to all the kids in the world, I would say, 'If you have a problem and you think drugs will solve it, guess again, they'll just give you another. And if you want to get somewhere in life, stay in school.'"

Tiffany, 13
Mesa, Arizona

Purpose
Raise awareness about how illegal drug use is portrayed in the *media* and the health issues related to illegal drugs.

Goals
▸ Describe some illegal drugs.
▸ Apply information about health and social problems linked to illegal drug use to personal life choices.

Teacher Preparation
1. Gather reference materials that contain information about illegal drugs, such as electronic and/or nonelectronic encyclopedias, health books, etc.
2. Provide *Internet* access, if possible.

Activities
Have students:
▸ create a composite list of illegal drugs.
▸ each select one illegal drug and research the health and social problems that have been linked to its use; share the information with the class.
▸ read a print or *Internet* article about illegal drugs or drug use; share the information with the class.
▸ locate and discuss the lyrics of a popular song that contains a reference to illegal drug use.
  · in small groups, rewrite those song lyrics, replacing the drug reference with positive and prosocial words; share the new lyrics with the class
▸ speculate about reasons for drug use and create a composite list of them.
▸ create posters that depict people "before" and "after" extended drug use; display the posters in an elementary school setting.

92

‣ create *positive* slogans that are intended to discourage drug use; contact the student newspaper and request that one antidrug slogan be published in each edition of the newspaper to spread the word about the dangers of drug use.

‣ create a new superhero who champions the cause of a drug-free *society;* each small group then creates one comic strip episode; place all of the comic strips together into a comic book *format;* reproduce and distribute it to younger students; place a copy of the comic strip in the class scrapbook.

Extensions
Have students:

‣ use the Internet to access information about government programs intended to reduce or eliminate illegal drug use.

‣ create comic strips or single-frame political cartoons that depict the dangers of drug use.

‣ videotape a panel discussion with students of different ages discussing reasons they would never use drugs; air the videotape on a community-access cable channel or the school's closed-circuit TV system, or loan the videotape to teachers to show to their students.

‣ make a list of the illegal and legal drugs used in movies, music videos, or TV programs over a two-week period; share findings with the class.

Looking at Health Through the Eyes of Media

"If I had to send a message to all the kids of the world ... some of the things you could do is not to do drugs or alcohol. These things will hurt you, change you, and can make you die. They will keep you from the more important things in your life, like your family. Treat everyone like it's your last day to live, or their last day to live, because then you will try to be positive about everything. If I were to present this to the children of the world, I would go live on television around the world. I would make sure my speech has closed caption for the deaf, and I would ask that my message be heard by adults and children, because parents can show their children. Remember ... we learn from big people."

Shelly, 12
Lihue, Hawaii

Purpose
Raise awareness about health issues related to tobacco, alcohol, and illegal drug use and how these behaviors are portrayed in the *media*.

Goals
▸ *Evaluate* the economic impact of tobacco, alcohol, and drug use.
▸ Create a *positive message* to encourage proper care of the human body.

Teacher Preparation
Provide reference materials such as health books and electronic and/or nonelectronic encyclopedias that contain information on health issues related to tobacco, alcohol, and illegal drug use.

Activities
Have students:
▸ discuss books, movies, or TV programs that have depicted the dangers of alcohol, tobacco, or illegal drugs.
▸ research the estimated amount of money made selling illegal drugs.
▸ research the amount of money spent each year on tobacco and alcohol advertising; create a chart summarizing findings.
▸ conduct the "Attitudes Survey"; discuss the findings.
▸ discuss the ethics of making money by selling alcohol, tobacco, or drugs.
▸ invite someone who has struggled with alcohol, tobacco, or drug use to visit the class and share how the addiction began and how it impacted various aspects of life.

Reproducible
"Attitudes Survey"
(p. 96)

Resources
Selling Addiction—kit
(p. 150)
Internet Public Library—
Youth Health Section:
www.ipl.org/cgi-bin/
teen.db.out.pl?id=he0000
(p. 145)

Equipment
Internet access
(if available)

94

‣ in small groups *brainstorm* specific ways that newspapers and magazines, radio and TV, movies, music, and advertising messages can directly impact adult and teenage attitudes about alcohol, tobacco, and drug use.

‣ research why tobacco companies and some alcoholic beverage companies do not advertise on TV.

‣ research organizations and government programs that are involved in antismoking, antidrinking, and antidrug campaigns.

‣ each write a journal entry about their feelings when they saw someone affected by drugs or alcohol on TV, in a movie, or in real life.

‣ create positive slogans that would encourage the proper care of human bodies.

‣ design cartoon characters to be used with the positive slogans; select the best slogan and the best cartoon character to be used in a new positive campaign; offer the selected slogan and cartoon character to an appropriate not-for-profit health organization to encourage the development of a more positive campaign.

‣ create a list of misrepresentations, myths, or exaggerations that ads, movies, music, and TV programs tell the audience about smoking, drinking, and drugs; justify each list entry; place the list in the class scrapbook.

Extensions
Have students:

‣ visit an antismoking, antidrinking, or antidrug *website* on the Internet; collect information about their campaigns; share it with the class.

‣ write to a healthcare or medical organization to request information about maintaining a healthy body.

‣ invite a healthcare professional or drug awareness counselor to the class to answer students' questions about the human body.

‣ research solutions to alcohol, tobacco, and drug problems, such as rehabilitation centers, nicotine patches; design a brochure or website incorporating the information.

Name_____ **Date**_____

Unit 7
"Attitudes Survey"
Alcohol, Tobacco, and Drug Use

Ask five adults and five teenagers these questions:

1. Why do adults and teenagers use alcoholic beverages?

    _____

    _____

    _____

2. Why do adults and teenagers use tobacco products?

    _____

    _____

    _____

3. Why do adults and teenagers use illegal drugs?

    _____

    _____

    _____

4. Have you seen professional baseball players chewing tobacco? If so, what was your attitude about them chewing tobacco during baseball games?

    _____

    _____

    _____

5. Should alcohol, tobacco, and illegal drug use be portrayed in movies, TV programs, and music videos? ❏ Yes ❏ No Why/why not?

    _____

    _____

    _____

Thinking About Real People

"This picture shows kids holding rods with stars on the top. The background shows stars but you can see little rods on them. The path leads up to the stars. The kids with stars show their hope and what they can do because children are the future. The other stars show accomplishments of famous people and children reaching out to the stars. The path is like the road you choose to reach your goals. Anyone can take that path."

Elisa, 11
West Hills, California

Throughout history, *leaders* have generated social change. Some have chosen their leadership roles, but most arrived at their positions of power unintentionally and through circumstances beyond their control. Consider the leadership of Rosa Parks. In Montgomery, Alabama, in the 1950s, she was told to give up her bus seat for a white woman, but feeling tired and frustrated, she refused. Her determination caused others to stand up for their rights, and she was thrust into the limelight as a Black crusader. She is still regarded as a role model for those deprived of their inalienable rights. Who are present-day role models? Who do we behold as worthy, and why? Role models, leaders, and even celebrities have significant power over our lives and lifestyles, but what are the criteria used to determine their worth?

Children and teenagers are vulnerable to the glamour and power of *celebrity* status. A great deal of credence is given to the individual who makes an impression—whether it is in the world of entertainment, politics, sports, or news. Though the recognition factor of celebrities is powerful, it does not necessarily translate to worth. In addition, there is a great deal of pressure placed on successful minority figures like Michael Jordan, Oprah Winfrey, and Jimmy Smits, who then serve as role models for youth. Evaluating the reasons for celebrity and *hero* status, looking for character traits in role models, and selecting leaders who have *positive* and visionary insight is a lifelong challenge.

By gaining information about *society's* celebrities, heroes, and leaders; engaging in discussion and reflection; and acquiring higher-level thinking skills, students can judge who is worthy of their time and attention, and, most important, their allegiance.

The activities in this chapter will direct students to look beyond the pervasive images and sound bites to determine meaningful criteria for their leaders and role models.

What Is a Celebrity?

Purpose
Examine the celebrities portrayed in the *media* and the reasons they are well known.

Goals
▸ Define *celebrity*.
▸ List some celebrities and explain the reasons for their celebrity status.
▸ *Evaluate* whether being a celebrity equals being a "good" person.

Teacher Preparation
1. Become familiar with current celebrities.
2. Videotape several TV talk shows, interview programs, or news segments that feature celebrities.
3. Bring to class a variety of magazines for student use.

Activities
Have students:

▸ discuss the meaning of the word *celebrity*; use electronic or print dictionaries to compare it to the actual meaning; place the definition on the bulletin board.
▸ in small groups list some current celebrities.
▸ as a class create a composite celebrity list on butcher paper or a bulletin board, and continue to add names as they come up in discussions or assignments.
▸ individually complete the "Celebrity Survey" worksheet as a homework assignment; share the results in small groups.
▸ compare and contrast requirements for celebrity status with criteria for being a "good" person.
▸ in each small group choose one category, such as baseball, rock music, recent movies, or TV cartoons, and create a list of celebrities for that category; discuss what is actually known about them.
▸ bring magazine covers to class and create a collage or bulletin board with the people, characters, or animals that are featured on the covers; *analyze* the common denominators among those depicted.
▸ discuss whether a fictional character or a pet can be a celebrity.
▸ research whether famous people from history, such as Abraham Lincoln, Amelia Earhart, or Babe Ruth, were celebrities, and give explanations for the conclusions.

e-maiL

net search

heLP

Reproducible
"Celebrity Survey"
(p. 101)

Resource
Hollywood/Show Business:
www.mrshowbiz.com

Equipment
TV and VCR

▸ view the videotaped TV segments; discuss why each celebrity is well known; categorize the people featured; decide whether each is famous because of positive qualities or accomplishments.

▸ write a short story about a fictitious person, animal, or character who becomes a celebrity, giving the reasons for recognition; share the stories; select one to be featured on the school's *Internet* webpage or in a school publication.

▸ each create a list of requirements for personal role models; compare and contrast the definition of a *celebrity* with their requirements for a personal role model.

Extensions
Have students:

▸ invite a local celebrity to the class to discuss how celebrity status changes one's life.

▸ ask parents to discuss celebrities they remember who created a sensation in previous years; compile a class list; place the list in the class scrapbook on a page called "Yesterday's Celebrities."

▸ each write a letter to a celebrity to learn more about the person's background, feelings, work, or goals; share responses; determine whether the person is truly worthy of recognition.

▸ collect cereal boxes; cut out the characters, animals, or people who are featured on the cereal boxes; create a quiz using the images; administer the quiz to students, teachers, and parents to see how recognizable the characters, animals, or people are; discuss the results.

Name_____ **Date**_____

Unit 8
"Celebrity Survey"

Interview ten people and record their answers on the back of this paper.

1. Name:

    a famous sports figure _____

    a famous movie star _____

    a famous musician _____

    a famous comedian _____

    a famous politician _____

    a famous cartoon character _____

    a famous animal _____

    a famous leader from history _____

    a famous author_____

2. What does the word "celebrity" mean?

    _____

    _____

    _____

3. What do you think the qualities of a "good" person are?

    _____

    _____

    _____

4. Is a celebrity necessarily a "good" person or a role model? ❏ Yes ❏ No ❏ Not sure
    Why/why not? _____

    _____

    _____

    _____

What Is a Hero?

Purpose
Examine real and fictional *heroes* portrayed in print and electronic *media* and determine some character traits of heroes.

Goals
▸ Define *hero.*
▸ Examine some heroes from past, present, and *fiction* and describe the reasons for their hero label.

Teacher Preparation
1. Read aloud stories of real and fictional heroes during the week prior to this lesson.
2. Determine the origin of "hero" from Greek literature.

Reproducible
"Who's My Hero?"
(p. 104)

Activities

Have students:

▸ define the meaning of *hero;* use the dictionary to compare their definition with the actual meaning; place the definition of *hero* on a bulletin board.
▸ complete the "Who's My Hero?" worksheet as a homework assignment; share the results; draw conclusions.
▸ each select and read a biography or do research about a famous person; prepare and give a two-minute presentation delivered in the first person; have classmates guess who is being portrayed.
   · each draw a picture of that famous person
   · present a thirty-second argument for or against the person being considered a hero
   · have the class vote whether that person should be considered a hero
   · place the drawings of those people who the class decided should be remembered as heroes on the bulletin board under the definition of *hero*
   · analyze the character traits of those featured on the bulletin board
   · develop a list of common character traits of heroes
▸ discuss whether a fictional character or a pet can be a hero.
▸ discuss the requirements for someone to be labeled a hero.
▸ over a two-week period locate articles in print publications (such as *Reader's Digest*) or the *Internet* about people or animals who could be labeled heroes.

Resources
Beyond Blame:
Challenging Violence in
the Media—kit (p. 139):
Elementary Unit #7,
Middle School #4
"Heroes for Today"—
Reader's Digest
monthly feature
Heroes—curriculum
guide (p. 144)
Hurray for Heroes—
teacher resource book
(p. 144)

- share the articles with the group; *evaluate* which of these people or animals should be considered heroes; place the articles in the group scrapbook and label the section "Heroes."
- each select one hero from real life or fiction and create a "hero card" (like a baseball card) and show it to the class; place the "hero cards" in the class scrapbook.
- compare and contrast heroes and celebrities using one of the following methods: a written essay, a journal entry, a letter to the editor, a thirty-second radio spot, a TV *PSA*, or an online *message*.

Extensions

Have students:

- view a videotaped episode of the old TV programs, *Lassie* or *Rin Tin Tin,* or the movie *101 Dalmatians* and discuss the animals' role in the story.
- listen to a fiction story about a hero read aloud; list five character traits demonstrated by the story's hero.
- each read the newspaper over a one-week time period looking for at least one news story about a hero; then create five questions they would ask that hero if they were reporters covering the news story.
- invite community representatives to a panel discussion on the topic, "Who Are Today's Heroes?"

Name_____ **Date**_____

Unit 8
"Who's My Hero?"

1. A hero is someone who: _____
   _____
   _____

2. Some words I would use to describe a hero are: _____
   _____
   _____

3. I remember a book, TV show, comic book, online site, or movie that was about a hero. It was
   called _____.

   Here's what happened and what the hero did to resolve the situation: _____
   _____
   _____

4. Some other places I've seen heroes are: _____
   _____
   _____

5. Sometimes a hero is called a "superhero" because:_____
   _____
   _____

6. Here are the names of some "superheroes": _____
   _____
   _____

7. My real life hero is_____ because:
   _____
   _____
   _____

What Is a Leader?

"Follow your heart and you'll never go wrong. I would put my slogan on a hot air balloon and go around the world changing the sign into all languages."

Bryan, 10
Pittsford, New York

Purpose
Examine leadership roles of people portrayed in *media* and determine some character traits of leaders.

Goals
▸ Define *leader*.
▸ Compare and contrast leaders from past, present, and *fiction* and describe the characteristics or personality traits that made them leaders.

Teacher Preparation
1. Collect several age-appropriate stories about leaders.
2. During four or five class sessions prior to this lesson, read the selected stories about leaders aloud to the students.

Activities
Have students:
▸ define the word *leader;* compare their ideas to the definition in an electronic or nonelectronic dictionary; place the definition in the class scrapbook.
▸ view a film, video, TV show, or online area profiling a leader.
  · talk about the role and responsibilities of this leader
  · create a composite list of leadership traits on butcher paper or the chalk-board
  · place a copy of the list in the class scrapbook
  · in small groups discuss who the class or school leaders are, why they are leaders, and what traits on the list they exhibit
▸ ask parents and other adults for names of past and present leaders and how they were portrayed in the media.
  · each select one leader and over a one-week period, research that leader by completing the "A Look at a Leader" worksheet

Reproducible
"A Look at a Leader"
(p. 107)

Resources
Famous African Americans:
www.newton.mec.edu/
Franklin/Ambios2.htm
"Kids '94 Compilation Tape"—video (p. 145)

105

· in small groups select one leader and prepare a media presentation (e.g., a poster, a *multimedia* presentation, a videotaped or audiotaped interview, or a *storyboard* for a three-minute *documentary*) that will share the information with an *audience*

‣ discuss the role the media play in presenting leaders to the public.

‣ assume the role of a documentary maker; select one leader from history and justify why that leader should be featured in a documentary.

Extensions

Have students:

‣ share the presentations at a parent get-together; break into small groups to discuss specific characteristics or personality traits of leaders.

‣ select a local leader, such as the mayor or school principal; invite that person to the class to discuss leadership characteristics, roles, and responsibilities.

‣ develop a fable about leadership, and select one of the following *formats* to present it: a comic book, a *PSA*, a children's picture book, or a short children's TV program.

‣ each write an autobiography of themselves projected into the future as adult leaders, including the situations that required leadership and the characteristics or personality traits he/she demonstrated; share them with the class; place them in the class scrapbook.

‣ all receive the same scenario for a difficult situation, such as trouble on the school bus, and *brainstorm* ways a leader might resolve it.

‣ match the list of characteristics or personality traits of leaders that the class developed with those of specific leaders from history; post this information on the *Internet*.

Name_____ **Date**_____

Unit 8
"A Look at a Leader"

Choose one past or present leader and do research to complete this worksheet.

1. Write the name of the leader:

_____

2. List the dates the leader lived:

_____

3. Describe a specific situation that required leadership:

_____

_____

_____

4. Describe the leader's actions or decisions that demonstrated leadership:

_____

_____

_____

5. List characteristics or personality traits the leader demonstrated:

_____

_____

_____

6. React to this leader's actions or decisions:

_____

_____

_____

"If I would send a message, I would say, 'Remember one thing, we have the ability to succeed in anything we try.' Technology couldn't always be used because some kids don't have TVs or computers, or even electricity. But they can look up to the sky and see a kite flying. Yes. I would use a kite."

Kristin, 11
Amherst, Ohio

Overview

Your students will get the most out of this workbook if the activities in Steps 1 and 2 are followed with a student-directed project. Why? Because the project will give students an opportunity to apply what they've learned about being discerning *media* "consumers" to becoming "creators" of media. This creative application of critical thinking skills not only reinforces students' learning but challenges them to expand their understanding.

The following discussion is a general summary of the theoretical underpinnings and benefits of project-based learning. If you are not familiar with this teaching approach, you may wish to read some of the materials referenced in this discussion.

The remainder of the chapter provides suggestions for guiding students through the process of designing and producing their own media *messages*.

Teaching Methodologies of Project-Based Learning

What's a Project?

Well-known educator Lilian Katz explains, "A project is an in-depth investigation of a topic worth learning more about. The investigation is usually undertaken by a small group of children within a class, sometimes the whole class and occasionally by an individual child ... the goal of a project is to learn more about the topic rather than to seek right answers to questions posed by the teacher."[1]

Using projects in the classroom is not a new idea; it dates back at least to the 1920s when it became popularized through the work of John Dewey and others. Over the years, project-based learning has taken on different forms and terms, such as *"constructivist"* or "hands–on" instruction and "problem–solving" or "performance–based" education, each of which have their own particular implications in the way the theory is applied to classroom instruction. Whatever you want to call it, many K–12 educators over the years have discovered that interdisciplinary project work helps students apply or acquire new information that supplements concepts taught with more traditional teaching methods, such as "chalk and talk" sessions.

Why Use Projects?

Project–based learning is sometimes called "experiential" learning. That term may make it easier to grasp the relevance of classroom projects: learning from experience. Project work gives students "the opportunity not only to be a part of the situation but also to relate to the issues and concepts ... learning takes on a holistic framework, working through multisensory channels."[2]

In classrooms with a multicultural or heterogeneous mix of students learning at different rates with diverse abilities, the reasons to use project–based learning become more urgent. "Standard, time–worn methods [lecture] are not good enough for non–standard students, the ones whose mother tongue is not English, the ones who grow up in poverty, the tragic new generation of 'crack' babies and those with fetal alcohol syndrome, as well as the learning disabled. They all require help in establishing the pegs on which to hang information. They all require more experiential education."[3]

Additional benefits of project work are realized when cooperative learning techniques–small group work, cross–age and peer tutoring, etc.–are incorporated to give students opportunities to develop skills in *interactive* collaboration. When projects also incorporate the use of technology tools, students not only gain access to a broader range of information sources but benefit from acquiring technical skills that prepare them for future learning and work experiences.

What's a Student-Directed Project?

An essential element of effective project–based learning is to let students select the topic(s) and direct their own projects–from start to finish. This not only motivates students but boosts their self-esteem with a feeling of ownership. "Schools are often places where students engage in activities of someone else's choosing which they find neither interesting nor compelling. In these situations, students may actively resist learning ... projects are seen as a way of engaging students in activities that they can own ... students will learn as a result of their own desires to do and to know."[4]

Self-directed projects involve students in making decisions and choices that affect the outcome of their endeavors–providing experience with cause/effect relationships. Because the relationship between effort and outcome is learned firsthand, self–directed projects help students learn to be more responsible for their own work and for the work of their group.

What About Skills Transfer?

When considering the worth of any educational endeavor it's important to consider the question of *transfer:* Will students be able to use skills learned in one context in a different context when the need arises?

At its best, experiential learning helps students use their intuition and academic skills in meaningful activities "where techniques of observation and reflection are brought into the learning experience to expand and stimulate a student's understanding of underlying principles and theories that can be re-applied creatively to new situations."[5] In projects involving creating media messages, students first employ "observation and reflection" on the content and form of media messages, which is a prerequisite to being able to produce one. They have had practice doing this in the activities in Steps 1 and 2 of this workbook. As they proceed to conceptualizing and producing a media message of their own, the underlying educational principle–that media messages are constructed by making deliberate and selective choices–will be experienced and understood on a deeper level. The goal of the project is for students to transfer or reapply this newfound understanding to the media messages they encounter in their everyday lives. That's what *new media literacy* is all about.

With that aim in mind, let the project begin!

Creating Media Messages

"If I could send any message to the kids all over the world, I would say, 'There are no shortcuts.' If I had access to all the communications technology in the world I would send my message by going into space in a ship and carve my message on the moon and whenever there's a full moon you will see it."

Concepcion Ortiz, 13
Houston, Texas

The Project Process

Impromptu activities can enliven classroom learning, but unplanned projects can be disruptive. That doesn't mean every detail needs to be worked out ahead of time. It's important to leave room for making changes along the way as new ideas are sparked by the creative process. There are, however, some guidelines that can help you and your students stay on track and allow for unplanned excursions in learning.

Process Guidelines

To keep the project fluid and dynamic yet manageable, it's helpful for you and your students to be in agreement about the overall project process. Two examples for structuring student projects are provided: "The Big Six"[6] and "Project Design Process"[7] (see pp. 123 and 121). Reproduce and distribute either one of these, or another process model you wish to use, and discuss it with the class. Answer questions students may have about the process before the project begins.

Materials

The form of the media messages your students will create will vary according to the materials and resources used. Discuss media resources that are available in your classroom, school media center, and *community*.

Encourage students to use as many different types of media as possible, including text (typewritten or word processed); art (drawings, paintings, photographs, or technical illustrations); music and/or *sound effects* (recorded or original); narrations; *animations*; and video.

Schedule

Work with your students to establish a schedule so they will know how much time they have to complete their projects (see Shared Decision Making sidebar, p. 117). Reproducing and discussing the schedule with older students gives them an opportunity to learn about deadlines and the importance of managing their time. With younger students, who generally have more difficulty estimating time, it may be more meaningful to provide direct guidance as the project progresses.

If you and your students embark on a project that involves learning how to use new technology tools—whether it's a *DAT* machine, *videocamera* or *HTML* coding for webpages—be sure to allow time for them to "play with" or experiment with the new learning tools.

The project schedule will vary according to the complexity of the task (see "Sample Project Schedule," pp. 126–127, which you can use or adapt).

Expectations

It's helpful for students to know how their projects will be assessed before the project begins. What constitutes a good project? Because this is a self-directed project, you may want to negotiate the evaluation criteria together with your students and have them help decide how much weight is given to each criterion. As Alfie Kohn recommends in "Choices for Children," "Students ought to help determine the criteria by which their work will be judged and then play a role in weighing their work against those criteria. This achieves several things at once: it gives students more control over their education, it makes evaluation feel less punitive, and it provides an important learning experience in itself."[8]

Here are a few questions to guide the process of determining evaluation criteria. Is it more important that:

- ▸ the product is well-planned?
- ▸ the product reflects skill and quality production?

> ▸ the students cooperate with teammates?
> ▸ the students are considerate of individual abilities and differences?
> ▸ the students master new technology skills?
> ▸ the students do a good job of demonstrating what they have learned in their final presentation?

If your students aren't involved in the process of establishing the evaluation criteria, share your expectations with them before the project begins. As noted in "Assessing the Big Outcomes," "Knowing the assessment criteria up front, students take responsibility for becoming prepared and use their teacher as resource and coach."[9]

Getting Started
A good way to inspire the creation of a wide variety of student-created media messages and to help students connect their message within the goals of the class project is to use a thematic approach.

Determining Themes
Themes can be proposed by either you or your students. Ideally, the topics will be broad enough to integrate with other academic subjects students are currently studying (see Curriculum Matrix, p. 10). The goal is to have students *brainstorm* and select themes that help them personally relate media messages to their everyday lives.

One approach to brainstorming (see sidebar, p. 113) is to establish one or more themes, then have students break into teams to create their message(s) around the theme(s). An alternative method would be to ask students to bring in messages that interest them and see what common themes develop, then narrow down the list.

Using this method, follow or modify these procedures according to age abilities or other variables:

> ▸ To generate topics for discussion, students can use either the message from their "Create or Change the Message" worksheet that they completed in Step 1 (p. 50) or create a different message. In either case, have students complete the "My Team" (p. 122) worksheet as a homework assignment.
> ▸ At the next class session, students take turns sharing their messages orally, then brainstorm together to identify and select common themes, such as education or health, expressed in their various messages.
> ▸ Review themes gathered during the brainstorming session. Consider individual interests and skills indicated on the "My Team" worksheet to group students into teams (see "Small-Group Teams section" p. 114).
> ▸ Students work in teams to make the final decision about the message they will create. They can choose to select one of the messages already suggested by one of their teammates, or they can work together or individually to create a new message, based on the theme.

Sample Project Ideas

If you or your students have difficulty generating class project ideas of your own, see "Sample Media Project Descriptions" (pp. 128–133). These suggestions are meant to give you a general idea about the nature of student–directed projects–ones that engage students on a long–term, complex level. If you or your students have little or no experience with project–based learning, try a simpler project first, then tackle a more challenging one.

Remember: After you've considered available resources and identified which projects would be possible, let students either select the project that interests them most or originate a media message project idea of their own.

Working in Teams

"If we expect students to work together, we must teach them social skills just as purposefully and precisely as we teach them academic skills."[10]

To accomplish work in project teams, students need to agree on what they want to accomplish and how they will get the job done.

As students work together to decide the content and form of their media message and how to produce it, conflicts may arise. Students may not be experienced in setting mutual goals and in making compromises about personal feelings to accomplish group tasks. However, through practice and encouragement, they can become aware of and proficient at applying appropriate behaviors that facilitate group work. In the process, they will be developing interpersonal skills that will serve them well in all aspects of their lives–in school, at home, and later, in their career.

It will be helpful to discuss the following techniques before beginning the project.

Interpersonal Skills

Explain and discuss *Teamwork!* goals, which were derived from research and writings in the fields of industrial teamwork and problem solving.[11] Have students come up in front of the class in pairs or groups of three to model or act out examples of the action words at the beginning of each

Brainstorming

There are many ways to brainstorm; the exact method used is less important than making sure all aspects of the process are completed, namely:

‣ Generating ideas. It's best when everyone takes a turn participating ("passing" is okay). All ideas are welcome; no idea is criticized. Ideas are recorded on a blackboard or flip chart for everyone to see.

‣ Reviewing the list to clarify concepts. It's helpful to make a concept map showing a web or matrix of the topic and associated subtopics. Also list resources available in the classroom and community.

‣ Evaluating the list to eliminate duplications, topics that are off-limits, and so forth.

‣ Discussing and narrowing down the list by consensus or voting.

Good questions to stimulate a dialogue with students during brainstorming sessions are, "What do you know about this?" "What more would you like to know?" "Where could you find more information?"

goal. If students need direction for their impromptu dramatizations, ask questions such as, "What is the situation? What would you be doing or saying?" "What would it look like?" "What would your attitude be?" and so forth.

Teamwork! Goals

1. **Listen** to your teacher and other teammates.
2. **Communicate** your thoughts and feelings.
3. **Plan** what you do with teammates.
4. **Work** diligently at your own job.
5. **Ask** teammates for help when it is needed.
6. **Help** and encourage teammates.
7. **Evaluate** your progress regularly with teammates.

You may wish to make a poster of *Teamwork!* goals and display it in your classroom as a reminder for students to follow *positive* behaviors as they work on their project.

Another technique your students will find useful in instances when conflicts escalate and their emotions or actions are out of control is the "stoplight" strategy, as cited in Daniel Goleman's *Emotional Intelligence*.[12] It provides a time-out process that encourages students to manage their emotional impulses, calm themselves enough to find a solution to the problem, and rejoin the team as a cooperative member.

Red light	1. Stop, calm down, and think before you act.
Yellow light	2. Say the problem and how you feel.
	3. Set a positive goal.
	4. Think of many solutions.
	5. Think ahead to the consequences.
Green light	6. Go ahead and try the best plan.

Discuss the stoplight process. Ask students to think of a problem and explain how it might be worked out. Again, a classroom poster can act as a positive reminder of how to productively cope with emotional impulses.

Small-Group Teams

Assign students to small-group teams. Ideally, these will be heterogeneous groups of three to five students, preferably an ethnic and gender mix with a range of learning styles and abilities.

Shared interests is another important consideration when assigning teams. Watch for common themes expressed by students during the brainstorming session.

Roles Within Teams

Within each group, students need to have both individual and group responsibilities. Either assign, or let older students select, job titles and roles. Specific titles and roles will depend on the nature of the project, but here are a few ideas:

Timekeeper:	watches schedule, makes sure group keeps on task to meet deadline.
Facilitator:	makes sure everyone in the group is participating and is heard.
Recorder:	writes down ideas and materials needed.
Research/Resource Manager:	researches, collects, and maintains a folder of resource materials, and returns materials.
Presenter:	shares the thinking and feelings of the team when the project is presented to the class.

Discuss the responsibilities of the various roles in a whole class discussion. Be sure that students understand that each member of their team is responsible for fulfilling their individual role as well as whatever responsibilities they take on in creating media for their group project. Alert students who are doing projects alone that they will need to assume responsibility for all of the roles in completing their media message.

Producing Media Messages

Before students start producing their media messages, have them use the "My Team" worksheet (p. 122)–or devise another means you may prefer–to record their theme, message(s), list of team members, and the role each will play on the team. Emphasize that this information must be submitted for your approval. This is an important checkpoint to be sure students have a clear idea of what their message is and a structure for working together before they proceed.

Storyboarding

Once students decide the content and wording of their message, they can proceed to storyboarding their ideas. A *storyboard* is a scene–by–scene depiction that will help students determine what media they will use, and plan how they will use it to communicate their message.

This process will be new to most students, so it will be important to hold a whole class instructional session on how to create a storyboard. The sample "Storyboard Template" (see p. 125) can be reproduced and distributed so students can refer to the worksheet as it's being discussed.

Explain to students that professional *directors* and *producers* of television movies and cartoons, motion pictures, video games, *CD-ROMs*, and *websites* use storyboards to help them make important planning decisions about elements in each scene.

Visuals. Who or what will be seen? Will it be in color or black and white? Will it be a moving or a static image? (Static images would include a drawing, illustration, or photograph; moving images could include animations or video.) If there's movement, what's happening? Will what's seen be real or imaginary?

Let students know they will be making rough sketches of the visual elements in their message in the box titled "See What?" on the storyboard worksheet. Explain that they will use a separate sheet for each scene. The quality of the sketch isn't important (stick figures are okay). It should, however, show all visual elements (people, animals, setting, props, etc.).

Audio. Will there be original or prerecorded background music or sound effects? If there's music, will it be instrumental or with lyrics? What will the lyrics say? Or will their message have a *voice-over* narration? If so, what will the narrator say?

Text. Will there be any words on the screen, such as a title or *captions*, like a silent movie? Let students know that they will write the words (script) that will be heard, or the text that will be seen, in the box titled "Say What?" on the storyboard worksheet.

After they complete their sketches of the sights and sounds for each scene, encourage students to go back and fill out all the information on each sheet.

1. Use the checklist on the left-hand side of the form to mark all the different types of media they will be producing for that scene.
2. Use the checklist on the right-hand side of the form to record who will be responsible for creating each piece of media for that scene.
3. Decide what needs to be done first, second, and so on. Set target dates for completing each scene.

This is a good time to remind students about the deadline on their project schedule. Depending on the schedule, you may wish to limit the number of storyboard scenes. For instance, in the pilot program we were working with middle school students who had limited project experience and had a short turnaround time for completing *multimedia* messages to be included on a CD–ROM. Each team was limited to storyboarding three scenes to represent their message: one each for the beginning, middle, and end.

Let students know that when they finish their storyboard they need to submit it for your approval before they proceed in creating the *media elements*. Check at that time to be sure they have clear and realistic goals about how they will produce their media message.

If you are using the Project Design Process (p. 121), have students present their storyboards to the class for additional *feedback* and ideas after your approval.

Production

While they are creating their media messages, students won't always be sitting in their seats. In one corner of the classroom they might be playing *CDs* to select a song they want to record for background music. Across the room another group might be word processing their headline text on the computer. Other students may be rehearsing a scene for a videotaping session. It will be noisy. You won't be in the same type of control as when you're lecturing–you'll be on cruise control.

You'll be circulating around the room, listening to and observing groups in action to see if they are working together cooperatively. You'll also be asking questions to check students' understanding and to engage them in *metacognitive* thinking. You might say, "I don't understand," and see how well the students can explain to you what they are doing. Other times, open-ended questions such as, "Why did you ... ?" "How did you go about ... " "What were you thinking when you ... " will help students reflect on their own thinking process. Questioning strategies also can be used to keep students stay on track such as, "Have you checked this with your teammates?" "Are you on schedule?" "What's next?" Or use other tactics that have worked well for you in helping students stay on task in past projects.

In student-directed projects, students take responsibility for making decisions about each step of the production process. Have them determine and find resources themselves, or use the "Sign Up for Help" on the "Sample Project Schedule" form (pp. 126–127) to arrange for assistance from you, the school resource librarian, media specialist, school technologist, or other adults willing to provide support. In essence, let the students design and produce the entire project from beginning to end. If you are used to being the "information provider" in your classroom, you may feel uncomfortable at

Shared Decision Making

Excerpted from "Choices for Children: Why and How to Let Students Decide."[13]

"On a range of issues, adults can participate—and circumscribe children's choices—in fundamentally different ways. To wit:

▸ The teacher may offer suggestions or guidance, questions and criticism, but leave the final choice to students.

▸ The teacher can narrow the number of possibilities from which students are permitted to choose.

▸ As a general rule, it's more important for students to generate different possibilities than merely to select one possibility from among those that have been set before them.

▸ The teacher may provide the parameters according to which decisions can be made, perhaps specifying the goal that has to be reached but inviting students to figure out how they want to get there. For example, 'It's important to me that no one in here feels scared that other people will laugh at him or her for saying something stupid. How do you think we can prevent that from happening?'

▸ A decision does not have to be thought of as something that teachers either make or turn over to students. Instead, it can be negotiated together."

first in giving students more autonomy. Refer to the Shared Decision Making sidebar (p. 117) for a variety of different approaches.

Likewise, encourage students to enlist the support of their peers in solving problems whenever possible. Provide explanations and counsel only as needed. "In general ... one should resist the temptation to jump in too early and put the students on the right path. An essential part of learning is finding out how to identify a path of inquiry and negotiate the path in collaboration with others."[14]

Most of all, let your students have fun. "Learning that work is fun is an attitude for a lifetime."[15] Doing something creative doesn't mean students aren't employing the critical thinking skills you want them to use. In fact,

> Critical thinking and creativity may be considered as two sides of the same coin—pennies, perhaps. Put all the pennies face up to study the creative facet of the process—the part that is involved in generating and organizing ideas; all pennies face down to study the critical facet of the process—the part that involves assessment and selection. A thousand dollars worth of pennies might be taken to represent all the decisions that are made during the process.[16]

Presenting and Assessing Projects

Give students practice in both demonstrating and assessing what they have learned. After they present their media messages, immediately follow up with an evaluation or "debriefing" about the quality of the product, the process of developing it, and any other evaluation criteria you established at the beginning of the project (see Expectations, p. 111). You may wish to complete other forms of assessment later, but an on-the-spot performance assessment in a supportive and affirming atmosphere allows students to participate in evaluating their own work.

Classroom Presentations and Evaluations

The actual style of presentations of the students' media messages will vary depending on the form of the messages: dramatic portrayals; mocked-up newspapers or magazines with text, pictures, and photos; multimedia presentations with text, graphics, audio, videos, hypermedia, and so forth. The most wide-reaching *format* being messages communicated via webpages, which take advantage of the "unique features [that] the World Wide Web brings to this traditional and effective learning approach ... the ability to share (publish) learning projects with an audience in the tens of millions; and more importantly to the learning process, to build ongoing dialogues between the project authors and their audience."[17]

Whatever the form of their messages, do what you can to facilitate everyone being able to view each team's final product. Oral presentations are preferred because they give students practice in describing their work, verbalizing their ideas, and speaking in front of a group.

After each team presents their message, ask students on the team to remain in front of the class to answer questions or discuss comments from other students, or from you, about the information being communicated in the message. The following are some issues that might be helpful to explore.

- Could their peers determine the theme and message?
- Was the intended *audience* clear?
- Was the message complete?
- Was it well designed?
- What "worked" visually, what didn't?
- What was the best thing about it?

Consider other questions to help students reflect on the quality of their work. Facilitate this with gentle support, as some students can be insensitive to the feelings of others and oversensitive to the criticism of their peers.

While the team remains in front of the class, ask students to take turns talking about the steps they took to put the piece together. Have each of them describe the role they played. What was the easiest or most difficult part of working together? What could they have done better? What did they do well? Strive to end on a positive note. Repeat presentation and evaluation with each team.

After all teams have made their presentations, distribute one of the post–tests, pp. 18–25, and ask students to complete and turn it in. Also have them turn in their folders containing the worksheets, *surveys*, journals, and reaction papers from the media classes.

Once that's done, celebrate! At least, give students a pat on the back for completing their projects. You may want to have a small celebration party.

Additional Project Assessment
In addition to the performance–based assessment, you may want to consider the following items in your evaluation.

Portfolios. At the beginning of this program, students were asked to keep copies of their worksheets, journals, storyboards, and reaction papers in a folder. At the end of the project, ask students to write an introductory reflective letter to add to their portfolios. Have them state why they selected a particular message for their project; which classroom activities they participated in that they learned the most from (and what they learned); what they discovered about teamwork; and other self-evaluations based on the expectations mutually agreed upon at the beginning of the project.

Also, did they contribute to the class media scrapbook? If so, were their contributions on target with the subjects discussed? If it was original work, was it done well?

Evaluating Teamwork. Reproduce and distribute the *Teamwork!* Evaluation (p. 124) and ask students to fill out the self-evaluation form.[18] There's a place to enter your evaluation about the student's performance on the team. Also consider how well your students fulfilled their individual roles within the group.

Teacher Observations. Reflect upon your own observations about the way students worked together, the product they produced, and the way they talked about their project.

Pre- and Post-Tests. Administer one of the pre- and post-tests, which will give you a general gauge of what students knew prior to beginning your new media classes, and what new knowledge and awareness was gained from them (see pp. 18–25).

Community Presentations. If students have well-developed media messages, consider having them share their messages with others outside their classroom. For instance:

- in other classrooms at your school or at other schools
- at an after-school event at your school's library
- at a PTA meeting
- in the school newspaper
- at a local bookstore that sponsors community events
- at a local radio *station*
- on the school's website, if available

Have students brainstorm other places in the community where their media messages should be heard.

Name_____ **Date**_____

Step 3
"Project Design Process"*

1. Set criteria for the project

2. Brainstorm type of project

3. Write paragraph proposal

4. Have proposal conference with instructor

5. Present proposal, receive feedback, revise as necessary

6. Create a specific script, design brief or storyboard

7. Achieve script, design brief or storyboard approval from instructor

8. Research, resource, build and complete project

9. Present project

10. Participate in evaluation process

Step 3
"My Team"

Theme: _____

Who's on my team? (list all names and roles for each)   **Roles**

_____   _____

_____   _____

_____   _____

_____   _____

> **REMEMBER:** No more than two messages per group; just one is OK.

Select ONE of the options below:

OPTION A: One Message

Message:

(all names listed above will create this message)

OPTION B: Two Messages

Message:

Message:

Who will create this message?

Who will create this message?

_____   _____

_____

_____

OPTION C: Two Messages

Message:

Message:

Who will create this message?

Who will create this message?

_____   _____

_____   _____

Name_____ **Date**_____

Step 3
"The Big Six"*

1. Task Definition
   - ▸ Define the task
   - ▸ Identify the information needed to do the task

2. Information Seeking Strategies
   - ▸ Brainstorm all possible sources
   - ▸ Select the best sources

3. Location and Access
   - ▸ Locate sources
   - ▸ Find information within sources

4. Use of Information
   - ▸ Engage (read, hear, view, or touch)
   - ▸ Take out needed information

5. Synthesis
   - ▸ Organize information from all sources
   - ▸ Create product or performance

6. Evaluation
   - ▸ Judge the product or performance
   - ▸ Judge the process (efficiency)

* Courtesy Michael Eisenberg, © 1995

Name_____ **Date**_____

Step 3
*Teamwork! Evaluation**

At the end of the project, write a number for each item below to show how well you did.

0 or 1 = poor
2 or 3 = weak
4, 5 or 6 = fair
7 or 8 = good
9 or 10 = great!

Ratings	**Student's**	**Teacher's**
1. Listen to your teacher and other teammates?	_____	_____
2. Communicate your thoughts and feelings?	_____	_____
3. Plan what you do with teammates?	_____	_____
4. Work diligently at your own job(s)?	_____	_____
5. Ask teammates for help when it is needed?	_____	_____
6. Help and encourage teammates?	_____	_____
7. Evaluate your progress regularly with teammates?	_____	_____
Total scores for this project	_____	_____

What was one of your best teamwork actions?

_____

_____

_____

How can you improve in your teamwork?

_____

_____

_____

Your teacher may want to comment here or to discuss your results with you.

_____

_____

_____

*Courtesy Keith Beery, © 1997

"Storyboard Template"

Theme: _____

Media: ☐ Music ☐ Video ☐ Graphics ☐ Words ☐ Animation

SEE WHAT?

SAY WHAT?

" _____ "

☐ Voice Over
☐ Text

CREATE:
(What to Do)

☐ Music
☐ Sound Effects
☐ Lyrics
☐ Acoustics
☐ Text
☐ Essay
☐ Narration
☐ Story
☐ Poem
☐ Rap

☐ Photos ☐ Original / ☐ Found/Archival
☐ Art ☐ Original / ☐ Found/Archival
☐ Animation ☐ Original / ☐ Found/Archival
☐ Comics ☐ Original / ☐ Found/Archival
☐ Video ☐ Original / ☐ Found/Archival
☐ Film ☐ Original / ☐ Found/Archival

☐ _____ ☐ _____ ☐ _____

PLAN
(What You Do)

By Whom?
By When?

☐ Decide _____
☐ Design _____
☐ Write _____
☐ Record _____
☐ Coordinate _____
☐ Create _____
☐ Confirm _____
☐ Film _____
☐ Draw _____
☐ Schedule _____
☐ Bring (to class) _____
☐ Check w/Group _____
☐ Brainstorm _____
☐ _____
☐ _____
☐ _____
☐ _____
☐ _____
☐ _____

"Sample Project Schedule"

MAY

MON	TUES	WED	THURS	FRI	SAT	SUN
				3		
	Class 4 14			10		
				Class 5 17		
				Class 6 24		
				Class 7 31		

JUNE

MON	TUES	WED	THURS	FRI	SAT	SUN
				Class 8 7		
				Class 9 14		

What Needs to Be Done?	Who's Going to Do It?	Sign Up for Help with Professional	Begin	Deadline
Join Group			Class 4	Class 5
Decide Message			Class 4	Class 5
Storyboard				
☐ Create and Complete			Class 5	Class 6
☐ Approved				Class 6
Create Media: TEXT Be sure "Say What" is completed on each page of storyboard and decide how to convey the words:			Class 5	
a) Are words to be seen? Word Process on Computer			Class 6	Class 7
b) Are words to be heard? Record on Microphone		☐ Sign up ☐ Date _____	Class 6	Class 7
SOUND (Audio) Effects or Acoustics				
☐ Create original		☐ Sign up ☐ Date _____	Class 6	Class 7
☐ Record from existing			Class 6	Class 7
Music				
☐ Create original		☐ Sign up ☐ Date _____	Class 6	Class 7
☐ Record from existing			Class 6	Class 7

"Sample Project Schedule" page 2

What Needs to Be Done?	Who's Going to Do It?	Sign-Up for Help with Professional	Begin	Deadline
IMAGES				
Drawings or Paintings				
☐ Create original			Class 6	Class 7
☐ Scan		☐ Sign up ☐ Date ___	Class 6	Class 7
Photographs				
☐ Create original			Class 6	Class 7
☐ Scan		☐ Sign up ☐ Date ___		
Comics				
☐ Create original			Class 6	Class 7
☐ Scan		☐ Sign up ☐ Date ___		
Animation				
☐ Create original		☐ Sign up ☐ Date ___	Class 6	Class 8
VIDEO				
☐ Create text (script)				
Be sure "Say What" is completed on each page of storyboard and decide how to convey the words.			Class 6	Class 7
☐ Create sound (audio)				
Effects or Acoustics				
☐ Create original		☐ Sign up ☐ Date ___	Class 6	Class 7
☐ Record from existing				
Music				
☐ Create original		☐ Sign up ☐ Date ___	Class 6	Class 7
☐ Record from existing				
Costumes?			Class 6	Class 7
Props?			Class 6	Class 7
Scenery?			Class 6	Class 8
☐ Shoot Videotape		☐ Sign up ☐ Date ___	Class 7	Class 7
FILM/TV				
☐ Record from TV show or movie			Class 6	Class 7

Sample Media Project Descriptions

"My message would be to never grow up. It seems that most adults have lost the ability to see anything that is wonderful and magical that this world has to offer, to see the world through a child's eye, keep every experience as exciting as the first.

I would communicate this message by creating a movie where the theme/plot reverses the time-line and an adult grows up to be a child."

Carl, 13
Halifax, Nova Scotia, Canada

1. Nonverbal Presentations

Students select a situation where spoken language is not an option (e.g., communicate with a person who speaks a different language or one who is deaf; make a silent movie). Then they create a message about something they think the person or audience ought to know.

▸ Students can communicate their message by (1) acting it out nonverbally, (2) drawing or painting one or more pictures without words, or (3) creating a visuals-only webpage.

▸ Enactments can include charades, pantomime, or hand signals; dance; using their bodies to form the individual letters in the message; drawing and coloring large cardboard animals that stand for the letters (alligator for "a," etc.) that they can hold and walk behind; or other methods students can think up. Enactments can be enhanced with instrumental music, clapping, sounds, or other *special effects*. If possible, videotape the performances.

▸ Drawings or paintings can be mounted on cardboard and set up in a museumlike gallery with each one numbered, so students can walk around with recording sheets (that they design) to write what they think is (1) the situation, (2) the message in each picture, and (3) any other items students think should be included. Discuss interpretations.

▸ Webpage(s) can include icons, drawings, paintings, photos, short segments of music, sounds effects, brief animations, short videos ... but no words!

Share the messages:

· with other classes.
· as part of a "Guess the Message" game at the school carnival.
· as a display at a local children's art gallery or community event.
· as a performance or slide show at a PTA meeting.
· as a "Hot List" webpage submittal to Yahooligans (see Appendix B, p. 155).

2. Song or Music Video

Students decide on a positive message directed to an audience of one or more, including young children, teenagers, adults, or the elderly. They may create one or more original song(s) or select prerecorded instrumental music to accompany and reinforce their message. Note: The lyrics of prerecorded songs cannot be substituted for messages students create in their own words.

Electronic Resources
Just Think Foundation:
www.justthink.org
Plugged In:
www.pluggedin.org
Studio for Art and Technology:
www.ybgstudio.org

Additional Resource
"Mama Don't Allow"—
Reading Rainbow
video series
(p. 146)

Students:

‣ decide and create the appropriate makeup, wardrobe, and stage setting, then perform the songs. If possible, videotape the performances. Discuss whether the visual images that accompanied the song helped communicate the message, and if so, how?

‣ compose or record two different songs designed to accompany one original, or prerecorded, video segment to create two different messages. Discuss how the different songs changed the meaning or affected the power of the message in the video.

Students can share their songs or music videos:

‣ on the school PA system or at school assemblies.

‣ with the intended *audience(s)* (e.g., if the message was directed to the elderly, students would plan a visit to senior citizen centers, private care homes, hospitals). Students decide appropriate places and contacts, then follow through with telephone calls, letters, etc. to make arrangements.

‣ at local closed-circuit TV or cable access TV stations.

3. Picture or Photo Contest

As a whole class, students decide upon and create one message (about a social issue or current event) that the contest pictures or photos will communicate.

Students:

‣ decide the information that needs to be on the contest entry form, such as a short description of the photo, why the photographer thinks it reflects the message, and any other contest rules, including the deadline. Then they design and word process the entry form.

‣ determine the criteria for judging the quality of the pictures or photos, such as use of color or whether the message was communicated effectively. Students decide how many "points" will be allotted to each scoring criterion.

‣ decide whether all members of the class will be judges or just a small group; if a group, determine how the judges will be selected.

‣ decide whether there will be prizes; if so, what will the awards will be and how will they be presented?

Each student creates and submits a contest entry, with a completed entry form. Students also coordinate the judging, tally the results, and plan the award presentations.

Share the message and the winning entries:

· at the school or local public library.
· at a meeting of a local media arts organization.
· with a locally based art or photography magazine.
· as a display for a local children's art gallery or community event.
· as a traditional or electronic slide show at a PTA meeting.
· by publishing them online.

Electronic Resources

MTV: www.mtv.com (preview content for age appropriateness)

Additional Resources

"Abiyoyo"—*Reading Rainbow*—video series (p. 139)

Electronic Resources

Classroom Connect: www.wentworth.com/classweb
Cyberkids: www.cyberkids.com (p. 141)
Online Visual Literacy Project (p. 148)

4. Slogan and Brochure
Students create an original slogan (message) about their school, town, or city. They produce a three-panel or multipage brochure–with text and drawings or photos–that incorporates the slogan.

Students:
▸ brainstorm five or more reasons why new students will like attending their school or living in their community; why sports, arts, technology, etc. should be supported in their school or community; or other areas of local interest.
▸ decide how they will communicate their slogan in words and images, and the resources they will use for researching and making the brochure.

Electronic Resources
Do Something
www.dosomething.org
Online search for
.com, .org, .gov
(p. 152)

Completed brochures can be sent with correspondence, composed by the students, to:
· local Chamber of Commerce.
· mayor and city council members.
· other local groups or national organizations selected by the students. Ask a local printer or designer to donate brochure mechanicals and/or printing so the local Chamber can distribute the student work.

5. "Op-Ed" Page for Student-Created Newspaper
Students decide on issues they feel strongly about and write *editorials* for one or more "op-ed" page(s) in a newspaper written by and for youngsters their age.

Students:
▸ brainstorm and select five or six themes of local, national, or international interest.
▸ decide who might write a "guest editorial" (a teacher, principal, or member of community, etc.), and outline how arrangements will be made to have that person (1) write the editorial, and (2) visit their class to share in the final presentation.
▸ decide on a headline for the "op-ed" page.
▸ decide on the final layout of the page from various ideas submitted.

Each student:
▸ picks one of the themes and writes a one-sentence message about it.
▸ either (1) writes an essay stating their message and explaining three or more reasons supporting their position, or (2) creates a cartoon or character sketch that incorporates and supports the message/statement.
▸ provides a rough sketch of the layout design for the "op-ed" page and submits it with the essay or artwork.

Share the completed "op-ed" page by:
- sending a copy to the school newspaper.
- sending a copy to local newspaper(s).
- sending a copy to appropriate community, national, or international organizations.
- publishing it on the class or school website.

6. Political Campaign and Opinion Poll

Students decide on a real or fictional candidate (e.g., mayor, school principal, dog catcher), then devise a campaign slogan and campaign strategies.

Students:
- determine platform issues (e.g., candidate for school principal might support shorter school days, different types of classes, or no homework).
- create a slogan for campaign buttons, T-shirts, bumper stickers, or posters.
- create a series of campaign ads (print, audio, video, or online).
- design an *opinion* poll, deciding "yes/no" questions to be asked to solicit people's opinions about the candidate's platform issues. Include three or more personal questions to be asked of the people polled (age, where they live, occupation, etc.). Polls can either be conducted using typed or word-processed forms or by videotaping interviews.
- tally the opinion poll results; use at least three different ways to visually chart the results.

Share the completed project by:
- publishing the results of the poll in the school newspaper.
- publishing all the campaign elements and poll result charts on the class or school website.

7. Print or Multimedia Magazine

Students identify and propose possible solutions to an environmental issue in their community about which they feel passionate or want to learn more. They research the topic and publish their findings in an electronic magazine.

Students:
- select one issue (e.g., acid rain, pollution, endangered species) that they think is most important.
- research historical data and current information in a variety of sources, including conducting interviews (videotape or audiotape, if possible); compare the data from different sources.
- take field trips to make and record observations by collecting samples, drawing pictures, taking photos, recording natural sounds, etc.
- compare field trip results with research data to draw conclusions and make predictions about the future.

Electronic Resources
CNN: www.cnn.com
The New York Times: www.nyt.com
FAIR (Fairness and Accuracy in Reporting) (p. 161)

Electronic Resources
Just Think Foundation's Political Poll: www.justthink.org/pancakepoll.html
The Internet Public Library—Presidents of the United States: www.ipl.org/ref/POTUS
Youth Vote Project: www.tedmondale.org/yvproject.html

> write a one-sentence message that is a call to action.

> compose or create articles, poems, games, videotaped editorials, etc. that are based on their research and include the message statement.

> select a title and design a cover for their magazine.

> create a table of contents.

> for print magazine: design page layout, paste-up pages, and bind with cover (contact local paper to donate press time or "gang" work by students with regular print run).

> for electronic magazine: learn how to use multimedia technology tools to create and compile media elements (see Appendix D, p. 173).

Electronic Resources

Multimedia Cookbook for Hyper Studio—CD-ROM (p. 147)
Greenpeace:
www.greenpeace.org
Lebuse's Letters—CD-ROM (p. 146)

Students determine how they will present their print or electronic magazines and make arrangements to share it at:

· the school library.

· a local bookstore or public library.

· a local closed-circuit TV station.

· local, national, and international environmental community organization(s).

8. Radio or TV Show

Students create a radio or television show like none they've ever seen or heard before–but would like to see. They decide the format, create a theme for the show, decide on one or more messages, and produce the show.

Students:

> research radio or TV listings to identify various formula show formats (e.g., TV game shows, soap operas, news, cartoon shows, radio talk shows, variety shows, such as *A Prairie Home Companion,* or sports coverage).

> discuss the various formula formats, then come up with an original concept that is different, including characters or features of the new format.

> decide the theme for the show and one or more message(s) that will be communicated.

> storyboard their ideas.

> produce the show, including writing the script, casting the characters, creating sound effects, etc. For the TV show, also design and make the stage setting, makeup, wardrobe, props, etc.

> rehearse and record or videotape the final performance.

Share the new radio or TV show with:

· local cable radio or television station(s).

· an educational film or media organization or event.

9. Multicultural Webpage

Students will conduct research via *e-mail* with students living in another country and publish how their preconceived ideas compare with real-life accounts.

Students:

- ‣ pick a town or city in a country located far away.
- ‣ decide how they will locate a sister school in that town or city.
- ‣ decide what they want to know about the day-to-day lives of students living there (e.g., what they eat, what they do for fun); identify the three biggest social problems facing the town or city in that part of the world (e.g., hunger, war, crime, clean water, housing, education, free speech); discover other things about which the students feel passionate or curious.
- ‣ compose a letter stating the purpose of their project and asking if the school will participate in the e-mail exchange.
- ‣ develop the questionnaire to send via e-mail.
- ‣ decide what they think the responses to the questionnaire will be.
- ‣ discuss the responses to the questionnaire received via e-mail from other students, compare with their preconceived notions, and draw conclusions from their investigation.
- ‣ formulate a message that summarizes their findings.
- ‣ create illustrated reports and/or taped interviews that state the message and provide supporting evidence.

Share their presentations:

- · with the sister school.
- · on a class or school website.
- · in a live chat session via the *Internet* or *America Online*.

"You can do anything if you put you mind to it. ... One person can make a difference. Let our generation be remembered for something phenomenal ... let's look (beyond) this world of racism to work cooperatively as brothers and sisters ... and construct a majestic future.

I would communicate my message through town meetings, radio, television, and the Internet with a celebrity spokesperson that kids widely admired."

Alia, 14
Tucson, Arizona

Electronic Resources:
PBS: www.pbs.org
NPR: www.npr.org
Nickelodeon:
www.nickelodeon.com

Additional Resource
"Making Grimm Movies"—video
(p. 146)

Electronic Resources
www.unesco.org
UNICEF: UNICEF Voices of Youth:
www.unicef.org/voy/learning/whole/wholhome.html

Additional Resources
Voices of Youth (p. 152)
SCAN: "Show #22"—video (p. 149)

NEXT STEPS

"My message to the children of the world would be that we control the future of the Earth and we need to protect, preserve and treat every living thing with respect so that future generations will have the chance to see all the wonders this world has to offer. The way I would want to present it would be through fireworks in each country all at the same time. Each message would be in the official language of the country, so that every child in every country could understand and start helping the Earth today. It would be so colorful that people from miles away would come to where the show was to see what it was all about. And also, this is one thing every child has in common ... we all live under the same sky."

Christine, 13
Hudson, Ohio

Your Future with New Media Literacy

Media literacy is the application of critical thinking to the *messages* in all *media.* Your students have had the opportunity during the introductory and issue-unit activities, as well as in their creative projects, to *analyze,* interpret, *evaluate,* and create messages. This is a highly motivating and engaging field of study and, no doubt, you've found your students eager to discuss, explore, and then produce media messages. Based on the insights you've gained and the *interactive* experiences of your students, you are now ready to become a media literacy advocate. Spread the word about the need for the integration of new literacy skills into other curriculum areas and into the *community.* There are numerous ways to get the word out.

> There is no one way to teach media literacy. The methods described in this workbook suggest just one approach—one we know works. That doesn't mean you and your students won't venture into unexplored creative territory with ideas and inspirations of your own. We encourage you to use them to shape the media literacy curriculum to your students' individual needs. "Trust your vision—bring your ideas and experiences."[1]

Administrative Support

Capitalize on your students' enthusiasm and the projects they've produced to introduce school administrators to the dynamic quality of the media literacy process. Invite them, as well as school district officials, to observe some learning activities, including student productions and panel discussions about media-related issues. Media literacy training can truly

134

look very different in different settings. It's important that the topics you've covered in your classroom setting are viewed as only a sample of this new field of study.

Budgeting concerns may become less of a problem if the administration endorses the integration of media literacy into existing curricula and understands its relevance to the students' decision-making process. Because critical thinking is not an additional subject area and can be integrated into all curriculum areas, it will be easier for the necessary budgeting of resources to be justified. There are media literacy conferences, organizations, *Internet* sites, and newsletters to help your school gather more information in order to stay abreast of recent research and teaching materials. The final section of this book lists many appropriate and inexpensive resources, such as videotapes, books, and kits, that can be purchased for the school's instructional materials library.

Peer Teaching

Sharing your ideas and success stories with colleagues may trigger enough interest to warrant an introductory workshop on media literacy. The staff development department at your school or school district may wish to offer a graduate course for teachers. In addition to formal workshops or classes, an occasional discussion group or *brainstorming* session about media-related issues may be appropriate.

The dialogue from media literacy enthusiasts can cause a ripple effect into the school and community. Consider facilitating an evening or after-school session to answer questions and formulate plans for future media literacy efforts. Share some positive student outcomes in a professional newsletter or at an educational conference. Other teachers will embrace this subject only when they have a clear understanding of its merit and see concrete results of such activities.

Student Organizations

Students may choose to continue their investigation, evaluation, and creation of media messages by establishing an after-school club or perhaps a more structured organization, such as a school radio *network*. The student council might offer a "Media Day," bringing in representatives from the print and electronic media to offer workshops or panel discussions on career choices, media ownership, advertising revenue, or other applicable topics.

Lunch discussion groups can be started. Some students may choose to become the school media reviewers and write or broadcast critiques of books, movies, video games, music, TV programs, or online sites. Bulletin boards with articles on media topics, comic strips about the media, or student-created messages could be placed in high-traffic areas. A school Intranet (schoolwide network site) or Internet *website* (with international connectivity) could contain media trivia contests, new research findings, or interviews with media professionals.

The media literacy theme has no limits, and students who are given the opportunity to explore and create will never look at media messages the same way again.

Community Awareness

Offer a workshop or a presentation at a PTA meeting, public library, or community service organization, discussing the long-term goals of teaching students to be independent thinkers. Most communities are concerned about the social issues that have been covered in the issue-units in this book but often don't know how to help children deal with the effects of the media. Media literacy gives hope to the community that their youth will give thoughtful consideration to issues that impact them now and in the future.

School subjects are often viewed by young people (and the general public) as irrelevant and dated. Incorporating *new media* literacy into all curricula will stimulate a new level of student interest. Learning about media messages can allow students to focus on popular culture in a meaningful way and make decisions about their lives based on reflection and higher-level thinking, rather than to be overwhelmed by media makers.

Link with arts councils, media production companies, and other media-related organizations in the local community. Bring artists to the classroom to enrich the media literacy program. Such community-based support can bridge the gap between the community and the school.

Media Outlets

The local newspaper, radio *station*, and TV outlets offer wonderful opportunities for learning. Visits to the facilities give a realistic look at the production aspect of media messages. Interviewing media professionals allows students to ask direct questions as well as investigate career possibilities. Make contact with various departments of the local media outlets to arrange for student internships or summer jobs.

Contact advertising agencies or public relations firms in the local community to discuss student activities and projects. Someone at the agency or firm may suggest an exciting idea that you would not have otherwise considered. Learn the name and phone number of the appropriate person to contact at each media outlet. If there is no possibility for tours or internships now, there could be in the future if you start an ongoing relationship with the appropriate people.

The local cable TV company has a community access TV channel that might be willing to air some student productions. If the school has a closed-circuit TV system, student productions can be broadcast to any of the classrooms.

Brainstorm with students or colleagues about other media connections, such as local magazines, or nearby university film, *mass communications*, or journalism departments. Make the contact even if it seems unlikely to be fruitful. Your connection may initiate a long-term association.

Consumer Feedback

Students and community members can give *feedback* to sponsors, media makers, and media outlets via *e-mail*, letters, and telephone calls. In Hollywood it is said that one letter equals ten thousand *audience* members, so don't be too quick to discount the effectiveness of a letter–writing campaign. It is appropriate to call the local TV or radio station with both *negative* and *positive* comments to remind them of their responsibility to serve the public. Teaching student or community activism can stimulate more feedback to media makers and may result in positive changes.

Staying Connected

The Internet represents countless possibilities for getting the word out about media literacy. There are national media literacy listservs (see Appendix B, p. 155), but a local one could be started to deal with school-related issues or community concerns. A teacher support group could focus on the topic of media literacy. A chat room might feature a discussion starter on a media topic, such as "Do ratings help parents with their teenager's music choices?" or "What *CD-ROMs* have you found to be exciting educational resources for fifth graders?" Connecting with teachers in other states or countries may result in new lessons or issues for discussion.

The Just Think Foundation maintains a website (www.justthink.org) with student projects, guides for parents, current affairs, and an ongoing dialogue on the topic of media literacy. The nonprofit organization's purpose is to encourage teachers, parents, and students to integrate media literacy into their daily lives. We look forward to interacting with you online!

"Abiyoyo"–*Reading Rainbows* video series
Looks at how music and dance can be used to tell stories.
Distributed by GPN (Great Plains National)
P.O. Box 80669
Lincoln, NE 68501–0669
(800) 228–4630

Act Against Violence Campaign
website: www.krma.org/aav/medialit.html

"The Ad and the Ego"–video
High school–level material. Examines advertising's impact on our culture of consumption.
Distributed by California Newsreel
149 Ninth Street/420
San Francisco, CA 94103
(415) 621–6196

alt.music.lyrics
Access to song lyrics from TV and movies. Students post their own songs on the site's news group.
website: www.geocities.com/SunsetStrip/Palms/3431/aml.html

Becoming an Active Citizen–kit
A component of *My America: Building a Democracy* video series. Provides an excellent overview of a complex topic; highly recommended.
New Castle Communications, Inc.
229 King Street
Chappaqua, NY 10514
(800) 723–1263

Beyond Blame: Challenging Violence in the Media–kit
Curriculum, leader's guide, and videos for children, teachers, and adults. Provides a practical and positive program to counter the proliferation of violent messages in the media.

Produced by Center for Media Literacy
4727 Wilshire Boulevard, Suite 403
Los Angeles, CA 90010
(800) 226–9494; (213) 931–4177
(213) 931–4474 (Fax)
website: websites.earthlink.net/~cml/cml.html

"The Bionic Bunny Show"–*Reading Rainbows* video series
Shows how media is created by looking at the special effects, directing, and editing of *Star Trek: The Next Generation.* For younger ages.
Distributed by GPN (Great Plains National)
P.O. Box 80669
Lincoln, NE 68501–0669
(800) 228–4630

"Breaking Through Stereotypes"–video, part of Yo-TV: A Guide to Video by Students for Students kit
A video–based package that helps adolescents learn to express their creativity and life perspective through video production.
Center for Media Literacy
4727 Wilshire Boulevard, Suite 403
Los Angeles, CA 90010
(800) 226–9494; (213) 931–4177
(213) 931–4474 (Fax)
website: websites.earthlink.net/~cml/cml.html

"Children in America's Schools"–video
Documentary by Bill Moyers, based on the book by Jonathan Kozol, *Savage Inequalities: Children in America's Schools;* demonstrates how the quality of education in America depends on the wealth of the community.
Distributed by SCETV Commission
SCETV Marketing Department
Box 11000
Columbus, SC 29211
(800) 553–7752

"Color Adjustment"–documentary
Traces more than forty years of turbulent race relations through the lens of prime–time entertainment.
Distributed by California Newsreel
149 Ninth Street/420
San Francisco, CA 94103
(415) 621–6196

Connect/Classroom Web
Site connects you with more than one thousand schools that have created websites on the Internet; will put school webpages on their server.
website: www.wentworth.com/classweb

"Connections 2: The Journey Continues" by James Burke–video
The *Connections* series, narrated by James Burke, connects a chain of seemingly unrelated events, people, and the process of social and technological change.
Distributed by Ambrose Video Publishing, Inc.
50 West Century Road
Paramus, NJ 07652
(800) 526–4663

Creating Critical TV Viewers–kit
This excellent curriculum guide and video introduce students to the making of the news and other topics that are informative and interesting.
Distributed by GPN (Great Plains National)
P.O. Box 80669
Lincoln, NE 68501–0669
(800) 228–4630

"Critical Viewing"–video
CD-ROM produced by kids, for kids.
Distributed by National Academy of TV Arts & Sciences
1550 Park Avenue West
Denver, CO 80218
(303) 863–8221

Cultural Reporter–software
This software helps students investigate important aspects of their community.
Tom Snyder Productions
80 Coolidge Hill Road
Watertown, MA 02172–2817
(800) 342–0236
website: www.teachtsp.com

Cyberkids
The "launchpad" section in this site has useful resource links to sites that help teachers and students get started on the Internet. Visit Adolescent Directory On Line (ADOL): education.indiana.edu/cas/adol/adol.html, Teaching with Technology: www.wam.umd.edu/~mlhall/teaching.html, and WebEd General Links for K–12: badger.state.wi.us/agencies/dpi/www/WebEd.html.
website: www.cyberkids.com

Decisions, Decisions: Prejudice–software
Distributed by The Bureau for At-Risk Youth
135 Dupont Street
P.O. Box 760
Plainview, NY 11803–0760
(800) 99-YOUTH
(516) 349-5521 (Fax)

Decisions, Decisions: Violence in the Media–software
Tom Snyder Productions
80 Coolidge Hill Road
Watertown, MA 02172–2817
(800) 342-0236
website: www.teachtsp.com

"Democracy in a Different Voice, a Video Lecture
with Lani Guinier"–video
Dialogue of democracy's meaning in a diverse society. For classroom discussion, the video can be viewed by section: "Silenced"; "The Tyranny of the Majority"; "Taking Turns"; "District of the Mind"; "Democracy in a Different Voice"; and "Speaking Out."
Distributed by Media Education Foundation
26 Center Street
Northampton, MA 01060
(413) 586-4170

The Democracy Project
A PBS online section offering information on democracy in the United States; contains the U.S. Constitution.
website: www.pbs.org/point/democracy/

Democracy Works
An online guide to individuals and organizations promoting greater understanding and tolerance in America and heightened awareness of threats to freedom of expression and civil liberties.
website: www.democracyworks.org

Democratic Values for the Digital Age–pamphlet
(See website for additional information.)
U.S. Presidents resource provides background election information.
Center for Democracy and Technology
1634 I Street NW, Eleventh Floor
Washington, DC 20006
(202) 637-9800
e-mail: info@cdt.org
website: www.cdt.org/

"DreamWorlds II: Desire, Sex, and Power in Music Video"–video
High school level material. Imagery from more than two hundred music
videos with narrative to educate viewers on the impact of sexual imagery in music videos. *Preview prior to using in the classroom. Violent content only
appropriate for certain students.*
Distributed by Media Education Foundation
26 Center Street
Northampton, MA 01060
(413) 586–4170

"ECO Spot, Power of One"
PSA about the power we all have to change the world in positive ways.
Produced by Kit Thomas
Earth Communications Office (ECO)
12100 Wilshire Boulevard, Suite 1950
Los Angeles, CA 90025
(310) 571–3141

E–Zines: Youth
A database to youth zines (electronic magazines) by youth for youth.
website: www.nerdworld.com/nw1697.html

FAIR (Fairness and Accuracy in Reporting)
website: www.igc.apc.org/fair

Fronske Health Center Health Education Brochures
A collection of informative essays on health–related topics, including
self–esteem, fitness, alcohol, drug use, and AIDS.
website: www.nau.edu/~fronske/broch.html

Frontline: "Does TV Kill?"
Discussion of different effects of TV on violence; follows three kids to
watch how they watch TV.
Produced by Michael McLeod
Distributed by WGBH
125 Western Avenue
Boston, MA 02134
(612) 492–2777

"The Furry News: How to Make a Newspaper"–*Reading Rainbow* video series
Looks at how newspapers are made, how the comic strip "Curtis" is drawn,
and how a student newspaper is created. May seem young at first, but
keep watching.
Distributed by GPN (Great Plains National)
P.O. Box 80669
Lincoln, NE 68501–0669
(800) 228–4630

Girl in America–Nike video series
Produced by Wieden and Kennedy, Inc.
320 South West Washington
Portland, OR 97204
(503) 228-4381

Girl Tech website
Girls chat about girls' issues, get the latest on girls' sports, learn about other girls' views, and link to various girls' zines.
website: www.girltech.com

"Harlem Diary: Nine Voices of Resilience"–video
Inner–city youth take up a videocamera to document their true stories.
Distributed by: Discovery Channel Video
Discovery Communications, Inc.
7700 Wisconsin Avenue
Bethesda, MD 20814
(301) 986-1999

Heroes–curriculum guide
This excellent resource emphasizes heroes and their attributes.
Teacher Created Materials
P.O. Box 1040
Huntington Beach, CA 92647
(800) 662-4321

"House of Girls"–video
High school–level material. Four teenage girls produce insightful videos. Marisa's piece analyzes the popular vision of beauty; Zoe's piece emphasizes the importance of positive women role models in the media; Maya's piece is a journey to meet a woman she admires, Maya Angelou.
Distributed by Independent Television Service
190 Fifth Street East, Suite 200
St. Paul, MN 55101
(612) 225-9035

Hurray for Heroes–teacher resource book
This book is a great resource for teachers with lists of books and activities to teach about heroes–both real and fictional.
Scarecrow Press
4720 Boston Way, Suite A
Lanham, MD 20706-4310
(800) 462-6420

In the Mix–TV series
An award-winning PBS series for and with teens. The website offers discussion questions, group activities, and resources that correspond to the programs and publishes stories written by youth on health issues, school, and art.
website: www.wnet.org

Internet Public Library–Presidents of the United States
website: www.ipl.org/ref/POTUS

Internet Public Library–Youth Health Section
Great resource site with links to health-related websites.
website: www.ipl.org/cgi-bin/teen/teen.db.out.pl?id=he0000

"Kids '94 Compilation Tape"–video
Video shorts produced by kids.
700 Series: *Heroes*
1300 Series: *Inventors*
1400 Series: *Role Models*
Distributed by Independent Television Service
190 Fifth Street East, Suite 200
St. Paul, MN 55101
(612) 225-9035

"Kids Talk TV: Inside/Out–A Media Literacy Curriculum for Ages 9 to 11"–video
Shows children how to be better television consumers, how to use television as a tool for learning, and how to make media of their own. Includes activity packets and guidebook.
Distributed by: United Church of Christ, Office of Communication
700 Prospect Avenue
Cleveland, OH 44115-1100
(216) 736-2222

"The Killing Screens," with George Gerbner–video
High school–level material. Looks at the effects of violence in the media on the individual's sense of security and relationship to community. *Preview prior to using in the classroom. Violent content only appropriate for certain students.*
Distributed by Media Education Foundation
26 Center Street
Northampton, MA 01060
(413) 586-4170

Lebuse's Letters–CD–ROM
True story of a grandmother and her two sisters who, desperate to reunite, write letters to stay close.
Distributed by Robert Linehan
Coremax Digital Renaissance
7831 Woodmont Avenue, Suite 388
Bethesda, MD 20814
(301) 854–1579

Living in the Image Culture–kit
Contains fifteen core modules with activities on the use of images in advertising, MTV, film, and cartoons. It focuses on how TV and other media influence our ideas, values, and our use of time and money.
Center for Media Literacy
4727 Wilshire Boulevard, Suite 403
Los Angeles, CA 90010
(800) 226–9494; (213) 931–4177
(213) 931–4474 (Fax)
website: websites.earthlink.net/~cml/cml.html

Magazines–*Disney Magazine, Ebony, Interactivity, Sassy, Seventeen, Sport Illustrated for Kids, Utne Reader, VIBE, YM Young & Modern, Yahoo Internet Life.*

"Making Grimm Movies"–video
Great explanation of movie making: scenery, acting, makeup, how camera shots are put together.
Distributed by Davenport Films
11324 Pearlstone Lane
Delaplane, VA 20144
(540) 592–3701

"Mama Don't Allow"–*Reading Rainbow* video series
How to create effects using music; inside a music studio.
Distributed by GPN (Great Plains National)
P.O. Box 80669
Lincoln, NE 68501–0669
(800) 228–4630

Marvel Comics–comic books
Comic book home of the X–Men, Spider Man, Wolverine, and The Incredible Hulk. Their website provides information on current and upcoming Marvel Comics and events.
Marvel Entertainment Group, Inc.
387 Park Avenue South
New York, NY 10016
(212) 696–0808
website: www.marvelcomics.com

Media Alert! 200 Activities to Create Media-Savvy Kids–book
This book is for adults working with preschool, elementary, middle, and high school kids. Great for an introduction to media literacy.
LMC Source
(800) 873–3043

"Media Literacy: The New Basic"–video
Literacy movement in your school district, city, or state. Renee Hobbs, Kathryn Montgomery, and Elizabeth Thoman share their experiences organizing grassroots media education campaigns for school districts.
Distributed by California Newsreel
149 Ninth Street/420
San Francisco, CA 94103
(415) 621–6196

Media Violence and Children: A Guide for Parents–brochure
National Association for the Education of Young Children (NAEYC)
1509 Sixteenth Street NW
Washington, DC 20036–1426
(800) 424–2460

Multimedia Cookbook for Hyper Studio–CD–ROM
Middle school students create a multimedia magazine about their community, and their teacher shows how they did it. Provides outline of tools and techniques.
Distributed by Mindscape
88 Roland Way
Novato, CA 94945
(415) 897–9900
(415) 897–8286 (Fax)

My America: Building a Democracy—video series
Covers important concepts in historical context and shows how they apply to today's communities. Comes with a resource directory disk in both English and Spanish.
Distributed by New Castle Communications, Inc.
229 King Street
Chappaqua, NY 10514
(800) 723-1263
(914) 238-8445 (Fax)

The Nation, June, 1996
Issue includes map of who controls media messages.

National Public Radio
Get access to public radio and TV program guide, program descriptions, transcripts, and online activities.
website: www.npr.org

Online Visual Literacy Project
Go on a tutorial tour of the many photographic elements that affect the meaning and message of photographs. Experience how shape, color, form, perspective, and tone give new meanings to photographs.
website: www.pomona.edu/visual-lit/intro/intro.html

"Open Your Mind"—video
Seven thirty-second PSAs made by teens for teens. Creative and thought-provoking segments focusing on teen issues like drugs, teen pregnancy, violence, and school.
Distributed by United Church of Christ, Office of Communication
700 Prospect Avenue
Cleveland, OH 44115-1100
(216) 736-2222

Passage to Vietnam—CD-ROM
In this interactive multimedia CD, seventy photojournalists take a photographic journey to Vietnam for the first time since the fall of Saigon.
ad•hoc Interactive
80 Liberty Ship Way, Suite 1
Sausalito, CA 94965
(415) 332-0180

Peace Talks–video series
Michael Pritchard educates kids about violence in our society, helps prevent violence by teaching kids how to avoid dangerous situations, and empowers teens to learn how to get along with others.
Distributed by The Bureau for At-Risk Youth
135 Dupont Street
P.O. Box 760
Plainview, NY 11803-0760
(800) 99-YOUTH
(516) 349-5521 (Fax)

The Public Mind: Image and Reality in America: "Consuming Images"–video
Bill Moyers documents the inundation of commercialized images in our society and the role they play in sealing off consumers' creativity and imagination.
Distributed by Films for the Humanities and Sciences
P.O. Box 2053
Princeton, NJ 08543
(800) 257-5126

"Recovering Bodies: Overcoming Eating Disorders"–video
High school–level material. The stories and testimonies of seven college students show the wide range of pressures that can lead to disordered eating as well as the variety of psychological and physical symptoms involved.
Distributed by Media Education Foundation
26 Center Street
Northampton, MA 01060
(413) 586-4170

Rights and Responsibilities–kit
A component of *My America: Building a Democracy* video series. Provides an excellent overview of a complex topic; highly recommended.
New Castle Communications, Inc.
229 King Street
Chappaqua, NY 10514
(800) 723-1263

SCAN: "Show #22"–video
Aborigine video conference.
Distributed by Globe TV
21 Girard Avenue
Sausalito, CA 94965
(415) 332-2020

Scanning Television: Videos for Media Literacy in Class—video series
Great up-to-date media literacy resources for students and adults. Includes forty video segments and a teacher's guide on topical issues in the media—from race and sex bias on TV to virtual reality and video billboards.
Distributed by Harcourt Brace and Company, Canada
55 Horner Avenue
Toronto, Ontario M8Z 4X6
Canada
(800) 387-7278

Selling Addiction—kit
An introductory program exposing the myths and deceptions of alcohol and tobacco advertising.
Center for Media Literacy
4727 Wilshire Boulevard, Suite 403
Los Angeles, CA 90010
(800) 226-9494; (213) 931-4177
(213) 931-4474 (Fax)
website: websites.earthlink.net/~cml/cml.html

"Selling Addiction"—video
An introductory program exposing the myths and deceptions of tobacco and alcohol advertising.
Produced by Center for Media Literacy
4727 Wilshire Boulevard, Suite 403
Los Angeles, CA 90010
(800) 226-9494; (213) 931-4177
(213) 931-4474 (Fax)
website: websites.earthlink.net/~cml/cml.html

"Slim Hopes: Advertising and the Obsession with Thinness"—video
High school–level material. Jean Kilbourne analyzes advertisements and offers a new way to think about eating disorders.
Distributed by Media Education Foundation
26 Center Street
Northampton, MA 01060
(413) 586-4170

"Smart Parent's Guide to TV Violence"–video
Milton Chen leads a program looking at TV violence and how parents can help kids become better viewers. Has great scenes of kids talking about how they have been affected by TV violence.
Distributed by KQED
2601 Mariposa Street
San Francisco, CA 94110
(415) 864–2000

"Smoke Alarm: The Unfiltered Truth"–video
This HBO special is an overview of how tobacco advertising attracts young people. Watch for it in the *Cable in the Classroom* magazine listings.
Cable in the Classroom
1900 North Beauregard Street, Suite 108
Alexandria, VA 22311
(703) 845–1400
(703) 845–1409 (Fax)
Educator Hotline: (800) 743–5355
website: www.ciconline.com

Straight Talk–CD–ROM
Twelve interviews with at-risk kids who gave up alcohol and drugs and redirected their focus on their education. Provides a glossary and "think-talk," an interactive discussion guide.
Distributed by Educational Resources
1550 Executive Drive
P.O. Box 1900
Elgin, IL 60121–1900
(847) 888–8300

"Teens Talk Jobs"–*In the Mix* video series
Includes information on how to write a resume and interview for a job. Great sample of teenagers playing role models. Other episodes: "Teen Talk AIDS"; "Teens Talk Violence."
Distributed by GPN (Great Plains National)
P.O. Box 80669–0669
Lincoln, NE 68501–0669
(800) 228–4630

Television: What's Behind What You See, by W. Carter Merbreier and Linda Capus Riley–book
This children's book offers a grand tour of the TV world.
Center for Media Literacy
4727 Wilshire Boulevard, Suite 403
Los Angeles, CA 90010
(800) 226-9494; (213) 931-4177
(213) 931-4474 (Fax)
website: websites.earthlink.net/~cml/cml.html

Time Magazine Multimedia Almanac–CD-ROM
Articles and quick-time movies through ten decades of *Time.* Sections on history, elections (1900–1992), and the environment.
Distributed by Educational Resources
1550 Executive Drive
P.O. Box 1900
Elgin, IL 60121–1900
(847) 888-8300

The TV Book: The Kids' Guide to Talking Back–book
This book speaks directly to kids (ages eight and up) to encourage critical television viewing skills.
Center for Media Literacy
4727 Wilshire Boulevard, Suite 403
Los Angeles, CA 90010
(800) 226-9494; (213) 931-4177
(213) 931-4474 (Fax)

"TV's Portrayal of Teenage Girls"–article
website: www.tvguide.com/tv/magazine/970127/ftr2a.sml

UNICEF
Discussions about online learning.
website: UNICEF Voices of Youth: www.unicef.org/voy/cgi–bin/discuss/discuss.cgi?/voy/research/disc2

Voices of Youth
The online UNICEF youth section where youth from around the world communicate online to discuss world affairs, share experiences, and build relationships.
website: www.unicef.org/voy

Websites: Check out sites that finish with .com, .org, .gov.
Have your students compare the messages of the slogans and websites of companies, nonprofit organizations, educational, and government pages.

What Is a Democracy?–kit
A component of *My America: Building a Democracy* video series. Provides an excellent overview of a complex topic; highly recommended.
New Castle Communications, Inc.
229 King Street
Chappaqua, NY 10514
(800) 723-1263

The White House
website: www.whitehouse.gov

"Woman" from Neneh Cherry's album *Man*–music video
produced by Virgin Records

"Woman Finding Love"; "Woman Getting It Off Her Chest"–Levi's video series
Series of animated commercials portraying women (clad in Levi's jeans) fulfilling their dreams and joyously expressing themselves.
Produced by Foote Cone and Belding
1255 Battery Street
San Francisco, CA 94111
(415) 398-5200

Women and Minorities on Television: A Study in Casting and Fate, by George Gerbner
Report to the Screen Actors Guild and the American Federation of Radio and Television Artists. Philadelphia, Pennsylvania, June 1993.

Yahooligans: www. yahoo.com (look for yahooligans)

Yo-TV: A Guide to Video by Students for Students–kit
Center for Media Literacy
4727 Wilshire Boulevard, Suite 403
Los Angeles, CA 90010
(800) 226-9494; (213) 931-4177
(213) 931-4474 (Fax)
website: websites.earthlink.net/~cml/cml.html

Youth Vote Project
Investigates what issues motivate young voters (ages eighteen to thirty). Students can review, learn, and get ideas from the project's polls, action plan, and results.
website: www.tedmondale.org/yvproject.html

Zillions magazine
See the April/May 1994 issue for the article "Are Video Games Too Violent?"
Zillions magazine is produced by Consumer Reports and often contains reports and articles about media topics aimed at upper elementary and middle school students.

APPENDIX B

American Center for Children's Television
400 East Touhy, Suite 260
Des Plaines, IL 60018
(847) 390–6499
(847) 390–9435 (Fax)
Strengthens the capabilities, insight, and motivation of children's media professionals; evolves guidelines and standards for recognizing outstanding work; increases public awareness and understanding of "quality" television.

American Medical Association (AMA)
515 North State Street
Chicago, IL 60610
(312) 464–5000
website: www.ama–assn.org
The AMA is a partnership of physicians and their professional associations dedicated to promoting the art and science of medicine and the betterment of public health.

American Psychological Association (APA)
750 First Street, NE
Washington, DC 20002–4242
(202) 336–5500
website: www.apa.org
The APA works to advance psychology as a science, as a profession, and as a means of promoting human welfare.

Ansel Adams Center for Photography
The Friends of Photography
250 Fourth Street
San Francisco, CA 94103
(415) 495–7000
(415) 495–8517 (Fax)
e-mail: fopexed@aol.com
The Friends of Photography Education Department offers visual literacy and photography classes to more than one hundred schools in San Francisco.

155

The Association for Media Literacy
40 McArthur Street Weston
Ontario M9P 3M7
Canada
(416) 394–6992
(416) 394–6991 (Fax)
website: interact.uoregon.edu/MediaLit/FA/MLAML
Provides a network for media literacy teachers throughout the world, organizes workshops and conferences, and publishes curriculum anthologies and other support material for media teachers.

Better Viewing: Your Family Guide to Television Worth Watching
CCI/Crosby Publishing
141 Portland Street, Suite 7100
Cambridge, MA 02139
(800) 216–2225 (for subscription)
A great magazine for kids, parents, and teachers providing guidance to what TV shows are out there and articles that look critically at different issues.

Black Entertainment Television
One BET Plaza
1900 W Place NE
Washington, DC 20018
(800) 229–2388
website: www.betnetworks.com
Music, sports, news, and pubic affairs programming.

Bravo
Community Relations
150 Crossways Park West
Woodbury, NY 11797
(516) 364–2222
International films, music, and performing arts.

Brøderbund Software, Inc.
500 Redwood Boulevard
Novato, CA 94948
(415) 382–4600 (product information)
(415) 382–4419 (Fax)
e-mail: education@pop.broder.com
website: www.broderbund.com
Software company specializing in educational software for use at home and at school, offering support for both regular and school edition software.

Businesses for Social Responsibility
1030 Fifteenth Street NW
Suite 1010
Washington, DC 20005
(202) 842-5400
(202) 842-3135 (Fax)
website: www.bsr.org
Provides information exchange on "best practices," practical business tools, educational seminars, research, publications, and topic-specific meetings on issues of corporate social responsibility.

Cable in the Classroom
1900 North Beauregard Street, Suite 108
Alexandria, VA 22311
(703) 845-1400
(703) 845-1409 (Fax)
Educator Hotline: (800) 743-5355
website: www.ciconline.com
Provides commercial-free programming in different subject areas for teachers to use in their classrooms. CIC publishes a magazine that contains program listings, articles about teachers who use cable programming, ideas on how to use television in the classroom, and creative ways to make the most of limited resources.

Cartoon Network
Turner Educational Services
1 CNN Center
Atlanta, GA 30348-5366
(800) 344-6219 (educators only)
(404) 827-1717 (general number)
Cartoon series and feature-length animation programming.

Center for Children and Technology (CCT)
EDF
610 West 112th Street
New York, NY 10025
(212) 633-8230
Policy studies, basic and applied research, formative research, and advanced prototype development with the general interest in improving education by altering circumstances in which teachers teach and students learn.

Center for Media and Public Affairs
2100 L Street NW, Suite 300
Washington, DC 20037
(202) 223–2942
website: www.proxicom.com/cmpa
Nonprofit organization that studies news and entertainment media using scientific content analysis; conducts surveys and focus groups to illuminate the media's role in structuring the public agenda.

Center for Media Education/Campaign for Kids' TV
1511 K Street NW, Suite 518
Washington, DC 20005
(202) 628–2620
(202) 628–2554 (Fax)
e-mail: cme@access.digex.net
website: tap.epn.org/cme/
Organizes and educates consumer groups and nonprofit organizations on issues of public policy and the media and publishes a quarterly newsletter called *InfoActive Kids*. CME's Campaign for Kids' TV works to improve the quality of children's television.

Center for Media Literacy
4727 Wilshire Boulevard, Suite 403
Los Angeles, CA 90010
(800) 226–9494; (213) 931–4177
(213) 931–4474 (Fax)
website: websites.earthlink.net/~cml/cml.html
Focuses on bringing media literacy education to every child, every school, and every home in North America.

CHALK (Communities in Harmony Advocating for Learning and Kids)
965 Mission Street, Suite 500
San Francisco, CA 94103
(415) 538–8580
(415) 538–8581 (Fax)
e-mail: info@chalk.org
website: www.virtualsummit.com/
A national nonprofit organization dedicated to getting communities more actively involved in public schools and in the lives of kids by using new technologies to facilitate community dialogue and inspire youth and adults to volunteer in their local communities.

Children Now: Children and the Media Program
1212 Broadway, Suite 530
Oakland, CA 94612
(800) CHILD–44; (510) 763–2444
(510) 763–1974 (Fax)
website: www.childrennow.org
A nonprofit, nonpartisan policy and advocacy organization that speaks
out for children in the legislature, in the media, and in the community.
Through research and communications strategies, they promote solutions
to improve the lives of America's children.

Children's Action Network
10951 West Pico Boulevard
Los Angeles, CA 90064
(310) 470–9599
(310) 474–9665 (Fax)
Informs the public about the needs of children and reaches millions of
people with examples of concrete actions individuals can take to make a
difference in children's lives.

Children's Defense Fund
25 E Street NW
Washington, DC 20001
(800) CDF–1200
website: www.childrensdefense.org
Works tirelessly at the state, local, and federal levels for just and decent
public policies for children and families.

Children's Video Report
335 Court Street, Suite 76
Brooklyn, NY 11231–4335
(718) 935–0600
(718) 243–0959 (Fax)
e-mail: CVReport@aol.com
A thematically organized newsletter reviewing and evaluating quality
children's videos.

Choosing Success
Computer Curriculum Corporation
1287 Lawrence Station Road
Sunnyvale, CA 94089
(800) 455–7910, ext. 6045
(408) 745–0285 (Fax)
An interactive multimedia curriculum to help students achieve success.
Through real–life scenarios, students learn thinking and problem–solving
skills to handle the issues they face in their own lives.

The Chronicle of Philanthropy
1255 Twenty-third Street NW
Washington, DC 20037
The newspaper for the nonprofit world.

Citizens for Media Literacy
34 Wall Street, Suite 407
Asheville, NC 28801
(704) 255-0182
(704) 254-2286 (Fax)
website: interact.uoregon.edu/MediaLit/FA/MLCitizens/HomePage
Activates progressive citizenship by helping people think critically about
the media environment to regain their powers of citizenship. Its members work with teachers and parents to activate the media literacy component of the K–12 critical skills curriculum.

Coalition for America's Children
e-mail: kids-info@cdinte.com
website: www.usakids.org/
The Coalition is an alliance of 350 national, state, and local nonprofit
organizations working together to call attention to the serious obstacles
impeding children's well-being and to boost children's concerns to the
top of the public policy agenda.

Computer Learning Foundation
2431 Park Boulevard
Palo Alto, CA 94306
(415) 327-3347
(415) 327-3349 (Fax)
e-mail: clf@computerlearning.org
website: www.computerlearning.org
Helps parents and educators use technology effectively with children at
home and at school.

Discovery Channel
7700 Wisconsin Avenue
Bethesda, MD 20814-3522
(800) 321-1832
website: www.discovery.com
Nature, science and technology, history, and global exploration documentary programming.

Do Something
423 West Fifty-fifth Street, Eighth Floor
New York, NY 10019
(212) 523-1175
(212) 582-1307 (Fax)
e-mail: dosomthng@aol.com
website: www.dosomething.org
A national nonprofit organization providing training, guidance, and financial resources to emerging young leaders of all backgrounds who are committed to building their communities. Special activities for K–12 students and teachers.

Fairness and Accuracy in Reporting (FAIR)
130 West Twenty-fifth Street
New York, NY 10001
(212) 633-6700
(212) 727-7668 (Fax)
FAIR is a national media watch group offering well-documented criticism in an effort to correct bias and imbalance. Publishes a bimonthly magazine called *EXTRA!*

Girls Incorporated
30 East Thirty-third Street
New York, NY 10016-5394
(212) 689-3700
(212) 683-1253 (Fax)
website: www.girlsinc.org
A national youth organization developing research-based informal education programs that encourage girls to take risks and master physical, intellectual, and emotional challenges.

Greenpeace Kids
1726 Commercial Drive
Vancouver, BC V5N 4A3
Canada
(800) 320-7183
website: www.greenpeacecanada.org/kids.html
Information on habitat destruction and endangered species.

Hawaii Education and Research Network (HERN)
2532 Correa Road
Honolulu, HI 96822
(808) 956-2777
(808) 956-5025 (Fax)
website: www.hern.hawaii.edu/hern
Explores the implementation and use of high-speed networking infra-structure to reform educational practice at all levels of public education in Hawaii. HERN has produced a series of media literacy videotapes of the courses, including *Film as Cultural Media, Internet as Media, Architecture as Media, Multimedia Production,* and others.

The History Channel
235 East Forty-fifth Street, Ninth Floor
New York, NY 10017
(212) 210-9780
website: www.historychannel.com
Historical documentaries, movies, and mini-series.

Institute for Alternative Journalism (IAJ)/AlterNet
77 Federal Street
San Francisco, CA 94107
(415) 284-1420
(415) 284-1414 (Fax)
e-mail: alternet@alternet.org
website: www.alternet.org
A nonprofit organization established to be an advocate for diversity of news opinions and analysis within media. AlterNet is a project of the Institute for Alternative Journalism.

The Internet Kids Yellow Pages
Website: www.well.com/user/polly/net-mom.updated.html
Search by subject for websites for kids.

The Just Think Foundation
39 Mesa, Suite 106
The Presidio
San Francisco, CA 94129
(415) 561-2900
(415) 561-2901 (Fax)
e-mail: think@justthink.org
website: www.justthink.org
Stimulates critical thinking about popular media by producing provoca-tive public service announcements encouraging kids to consider the impact of media on their lives and by designing educational curricula to equip young people with the literacy tools critical for the twenty-first century.

K–12
website: www.k12.org
Section index includes technology, nation, world, weather, business, entertainment, comics, tabloid, and sports.

The K–12 Daily Examiner
website: www.k12.org/k12daily.html

KidScreen magazine
Brunico Communications, Inc.
366 Adelaide Street West, Suite 500
Toronto, Ontario M5V 1R9
Canada

Knowledge TV
9697 East Mineral Avenue
Englewood, CO 80155–6612
(800) 777–MIND
Distance education, interactive field trips, language programming, and teacher training.

L.A. Youth
6030 Wilshire Boulevard, Suite 201
Los Angeles, CA 90036
(213) 938–9194
A youth news service written by and for youth. Reaches and involves inner–city youth, encourages teens to investigate issues that affect their lives, and offers hands–on learning experiences as an integral part of all programs.

LEAP Computer Learning Center
Leadership, Education and Athletics in Partnership
254 College Street, Suite 501
New Haven, CT 06510
(203) 773–0770
(203) 773–1695 (Fax)
website: www.leap.yale.edu/lclc
Offers computer and Internet classes to low–income youth. Get ideas online from their innovative and educational projects such as the online newsletters, the *Underground Railroad Experience* and *On the Road*.

The Learning Channel
7700 Wisconsin Avenue
Bethesda, MD 20814–3522
Offers history, science, human behavior, how–to, and children's programming.

Media Awareness Network
website: www.screen.com/mnet/eng
A support network for media education covering media issues, media education, and children and media.

Media Culture Review
The Institute for Alternative Journalism
Don Hazen, publisher
77 Federal Street
San Francisco, CA 94107
(415) 284–1420
(415) 284–1414 (Fax)
e–mail: alternet@alternet.org
website: www.mediademocracy.org/MediaCultureReview
An online publication of the best features, commentary, and criticism on media, technology, and culture from the alternative press and elsewhere.

Media Landscape
EDUCOMICS
Leonard Rifas
P.O. Box 45831
Seattle, WA 98145–0831
e–mail: rifas@earthlink.net

The Media Literacy Online Project
website: interact.uoregon.edu/MediaLit/HomePage
University of Oregon site offers links to many media literacy organiza–tions, government and media associations, and media resources.

MediaScope
12711 Ventura Boulevard, Suite 250
Studio City, CA 91604
(818) 508–2080
(818) 508–2088 (Fax)
website: www.mediascope.org
A nonprofit organization promoting constructive depictions of health and social issues in media, including film, television, music, and interactive games.

Missing Voices
Unlimited Productions, Sarah McNeill
17 First Avenue
Hove BN3 2FH
Sussex
United Kingdom
Global network of radio workshops for children.

MSNBC
2200 Fletcher Avenue
Fort Lee, NJ 07024
(201) 585–6469
A news, talk, and information network; Internet services.

National Association of Broadcasters (NAB)
1771 N Street NW
Washington, DC 20036
(202) 249–5400
e–mail: nabpubs@nab.org
website: www.nab.org
Represents the radio and television industries in Washington before Congress, federal agencies, the courts, and across the country. Their website is a great resource for information on many issues from a schedule of industry conferences to research and listings on subjects like children's television.

National Center for Learning Disabilities (NCLD)
381 Park Avenue South, Suite 1420
New York, NY 10016
(212) 545–7510
(212) 545–9665 (Fax)
Provides a wide range of programs and services designed to promote better understanding and acceptance of learning disabilities. Supplies information and referrals to local learning disabilities organizations.

National Education Media Network
655 Thirteenth Street
Oakland, CA 94612–1222
(510) 465–6885
(510) 465–2835 (Fax)
e–mail: NEMN@ aol.com
A nonprofit arts organization encouraging the production , funding, exhibition, and use of outstanding educational media.

New Mexico Media Literacy Project
6400 Wyoming NE
Albuquerque, NM 87109
(505) 828–3129
(505) 828–3320 (Fax)
e–mail: hizel@aa.edu
Publishes *The State of Media Education.*

Nickelodeon
Affiliate Marketing Department
1515 Broadway, Thirty-ninth Floor
New York, NY 10006
(212) 964-1663, ext. 126
website: www.nickelodeon.com
Entertainment and educational magazine shows for children ages two–fifteen.

PanMedia
759 Bridgeway
Sausalito, CA 94965
(415) 332-8502
(415) 332-8503 (Fax)
website: www.learn2.com
An "ability utility" website that provides information on how to accomplish many essential everyday tasks and skills. There are options to take easy step tutorials or request personalized tutorials targeted to your needs.

Plugged In
1923 University Avenue
East Palo Alto, CA 94303
(415) 322-1134
(415) 322-6147 (Fax)
website: www.pluggedin.org
A community computer access organization offering computer and Internet courses to adults and young people. Resourceful website for inspirational, creative, and high-tech project ideas.

Project Censored
Sonoma State University
Rohnert Park, CA 94928
(707) 664-2500
(707) 664-2108 (Fax)
e-mail: project.censored@sonoma.edu
Explores and investigates the extent of censorship in our society by locating stories about significant issues of which the public should be aware. The essential issue raised by the project is the failure of the mass media to provide the people with all the information they need to make informed decisions concerning their own lives.

Public Broadcasting Service
PBS Learning Services
1320 Braddock Place
Alexandria, VA 22314
East Coast: (800) 344–3337
West Coast: (800) 328–7271
PBS offers instructional, cultural, documentary, and news programming.

Social Studies School Service
10200 Jefferson Boulevard, Box 802
Culver City, CA 90232
(800) 421–4246
e–mail: Access@SocialStudies.com
website: socialstudies.com
Provides educational resources including books, CD–ROMs, videos, laserdiscs, software, charts, and posters. The website offers online resources, new media curriculum materials, and media literacy sample activities.

Strategies for Media Literacy, Inc.
P.O. Box 460910
San Francisco, CA 94146–0910
(415) 621–2911
e–mail: sml@fwl.edu
website: www.kqed.org/fromKQED/Cell/ml/home.html
Promotes media literacy, beginning in early elementary education; iden- tifies, develops, and produces media and education resources; conducts media education workshops; and serves as a center of support and con- tact for teachers of media.

Street–Level Youth Media
P.O. Box 578336
Chicago, IL 60657
(773) 862–5331
(773) 862–0754 (Fax)
e–mail: livewire@charlie.acc.iit.edu
website: www.iit.edu/~livewire/
Educates Chicago's at–risk youth in media arts and emerging technolo- gies for use in self–expression, communication, and social change. Offers classes in video production, computer art, and the Internet.

Telemedium, The Journal of Media Literacy
Produced by the National Telemedia Council
120 East Wilson Street
Madison, WI 53703
(608) 257–7714
The Council conducts workshops on family, television, and media literacy.

TV Guide
News America Publications, Inc.
100 Matsonfrod Road
Radnor, PA 19087–4525
website: www.tvguide.com

21st Century Teachers
e–mail: 21ct@21ct.org
website: www.21CT.org
Online network for teachers interested in technology; teachers share their expertise and access information on technology in the classroom.

WAM!
America's Kidz Network
Encore
5445 DTC Parkway, Suite 600
Englewood, CO 80111
(303) 771–7700
Programming on natural sciences, social studies, literature, and teen issues.

Working for Alternatives to Violence in Entertainment
105 Camino Teresa
Santa Fe, NM 87505
(505) 982–8882
(505) 982–6460 (Fax)
e–mail: future@rt66.com
website: www.rt66.com/~future
Develops feature films with new kinds of heroes and heroines wielding techniques and strategies more advanced than violence.

Yerba Buena Gardens Studio For Technology and the Arts
Fourth and Howard
San Francisco, CA 94103
(415) 422–0145
e–mail: info@ybgstudio.org
website: www.ybgstudio.org
A center for youth and educators that offers artistic experiences by introducing technology as a creative arts tool, resource, and network for communication. Includes creative, multimedia project ideas.

Youth Voice Collaborative
YWCA Boston
140 Clarendon Street
Boston, MA 02116
(617) 351–7639
(617) 351–7615 (Fax)
e–mail: yvco@aol.com
Assists Boston urban youth to analyze and shape the impact of media and technology on their lives and communities; creates opportunities for urban teens to interact with media professionals by coordinating internship projects in print, radio, television, and new media.

APPENDIX C

Useful Tools and Phone Numbers

This appendix contains information on the following electronic tools:

- ▸ **Animation software**
- ▸ **Authoring software**
- ▸ **CD-ROMs**
- ▸ **Digital cameras**
- ▸ **Imaging software**
- ▸ **Online services**
- ▸ **Recording device machine**
- ▸ **Scanners**
- ▸ **Sound editing software**

Adobe
Technical Support: (408) 986–6560
Sales: (800) 833–6687

Adobe Pagemaker
Technical Support: (206) 628–4501
Sales: (800) 628–2320

America Online
Technical Support: (703) 448–8700
Sales: (703) 448–8700

Apple Computer, Inc.
Technical Support: (800) 767–2775
Sales: (800) 795–1000

Brøderbund
Technical Support: (415) 382–4700
Sales: (800) 521–6263

Claris
Technical Support: (408) 727–9054
Sales: (800) 544–8554

Compton's
Technical Support: (800) 893–5458
Sales: (800) 862–2206

CompuServe
Technical Support: (800) 848–8199
Sales: (800) 848–8199

Digital, Inc.
Technical Support: (800) 344–4825
Sales: (800) 344–4825

Discovery Channel Multimedia
Technical Support: (800) 780–6044
Sales: (301) 986–1999

Disney Interactive
Technical Support: (800) 228–0988
Sales: (800) 688–1520

Grolier Interactive, Inc.
Technical Support: (800) 285–4534
Sales: (800) 285–4534

Hewlett–Packard
Technical Support: (800) 752–0900
Sales: (800) 752–0900

IBM Multimedia Studio
Sales: (800) 426–7235

Learning Company
Technical Support: (800) 852–2255
Sales: (800) 852–2255

Maxis
Technical Support: (510) 253–3755
Sales: (800) 33–MAXIS

Mindscape
(800) 231–3088
(415) 897–8286 (Fax)

Prodigy
Technical Support: (800) 776–3449
Sales: (800) 776–3449

Roger Wagner Publishing
Technical Support:
(800) HYPERSTUDIO
Sales: (619) 442–0522

Sun Microsystems
(510) 463–1133
(510) 463–1810 (Fax)

Time–Warner
Technical Support: (800) 565–8944
Sales: (800) 593–6334

Tom Snyder Productions, Inc.
Sales and Support: (800) 342–0236

Virgin Interactive Entertainment
Technical Support: (800) 874–4607
Sales: (800) 874–4607

APPENDIX D

Just Think Guide

Organizations like ours aren't the only ones that can promote media literacy. There are lots of easy things that you can do in your own home. We've combed through various publications such as *Telemedium*, *The State of Media Education*, and *Better Viewing* to come up with this collection of strategies you can use with your kids.

▸ Turn off the television during dinner. This will create a forum for family discussion in which you can take the time to tell your kids what's important to you and why you value certain ideals.

▸ Have your children read a book, then watch a movie or television adaptation and discuss how they are different. This not only gets kids thinking about media, but it can also provide some insight into the implications of different media. Why is it that the car chase took up only one page of the book, but accounted for five minutes of the movie? Why in the movie do we never learn about the main character's childhood, whereas it was a major part of the book?

▸ Keep a viewing diary to evaluate your family's TV time and see where you can balance and/or cut back. Try to keep a balanced diet. What's the ratio of entertainment programs to educational programs? Are you being selective about what you watch?

▸ Use kids' interest in televised sports to teach lessons about science and math. How does a pitcher make a ball curve? Why do quarterbacks spin the football when they throw it?

▸ Avoid putting a television in your child's room. A child with his or her own television gets the message that it's okay to view excessively and indiscriminately.

▸ Encourage your children to think about their favorite shows. Do they relate to the characters? Does the program represent real-life situations? Ask them to come up with alternate solutions to the conflicts presented in the program.

173

▸ Point out how media are constructed. Do your kids pay attention to commercials? Do they often remember them more than the programs? What kids often don't realize is that media exist to attract audiences for advertisers and programming is designed around attracting specific markets. The easiest way for children to begin to understand this is to have them pay attention to the types of commercials played during different programs. Why aren't there toy commercials during the evening news? Why are there so many ads for beer during sporting events?

▸ Recognize media stereotypes. Are they true? Are they false? Why? Try to compare the people you see in the media with people in real life. Can you think of any exceptions to the characterizations that you see?

▸ When watching television, make it a primary activity. When you watch TV—watch TV. Avoid making television the backdrop for other activities.

▸ Don't channel surf. This leads to a lot of unnecessary viewing. If you're having trouble finding something to watch, don't watch anything.

▸ Try to watch the same programs (or listen to same music, play the same games, etc.) as your kids. Chances are you won't find them as entertaining as your children do, but you will have a much better understanding of how your children think.

▸ Remember you are the master of the television. The standard defense of broadcasters against programming with questionable content is, "If you don't like what's on, then just don't watch it." It's not a bad idea.

▸ These suggestions can be adapted for children of almost any age. You can start as soon as your child becomes a media consumer (as young as two or three). The strategies we've suggested are great for guidance, but remember to recognize your children's independence, and allow them to make their own media decisions as they grow older.

▸ Finally, try to respect your children's culture. Just because you don't like your children's media choices doesn't necessarily mean they're bad ones.

Most parents spend 1,000 minutes/week watching TV and only 38 minutes/week talking to their kids.*

---

*The State of Media Education. A Publication of the New Mexico Media Literacy Project.

NOTES

Introduction

1. Victoria Neufeldt, ed. *Webster's New World Dictionary, Third College Edition* (New York: Simon & Schuster, 1988), p. 789.

2. John Chaffee, "Critical Thinking Skills: The Cornerstone of Developmental Education," *Journal of Developmental Education*, vol. 15, no. 3 (Spring 1992), p. 2.

3. George H. Hanford quoted in Richard Paul, *Critical Thinking: How to Prepare Students for a Rapidly Changing World* (Santa Rosa, Calif.: Foundation for Critical Thinking, 1995), back cover.

4. Victoria Neufeldt, ed. *Webster's New World Dictionary, Third College Edition* (New York: Simon & Schuster, 1988), p. 841.

5. Marshall McLuhan, *Understanding Media: The Extensions of Man* (New York: McGraw–Hill, 1964), p. 7.

6. E. B. White quoted in David Walsh, Ph.D., Larry S. Goldman, Ph.D., and Roger Brown, Ph.D., *Physician Guide to Media Violence* (Chicago: American Medical Association, 1996), p. 8.

7. David Walsh, Ph.D., Larry S. Goldman, Ph.D., and Roger Brown, Ph.D., *Physician Guide to Media Violence* (Chicago: American Medical Association, 1996), p. 9.

8. Paulette Thomas, "Show and Tell: Advertisers Take Pitches to Preschools," *The Wall Street Journal* (October 28, 1996), pp. B1, B5.

9. *Frontline:* "Does TV Kill?" (video). (Boston: WGBH Television).

10. Ibid.

11. David Walsh, Ph.D., Larry S. Goldman, Ph.D., and Roger Brown, Ph.D., *Physician Guide to Media Violence* (Chicago: American Medical Association, 1996), pp. 8, 9.

Basic Steps: How to Use This Book

1. Daniel Goleman, *Emotional Intelligence* (New York: Bantam Books, 1995), pp. 44–45.

Step 2: Issue-Oriented Units

1. Dr. David M. Considine, "An Introduction to Media Literacy," *Telemedium* (Fall 1995).

2. Marjorie C. Feinstein and Thomas L. Veenendall, "Using the Case Study Method to Teach Interpersonal Communication," *INQUIRY: Critical Thinking Across the Disciplines*, vol. 9, no. 3 (Institute for Critical Thinking, April 1992), p. 32.

Step 3: Media Projects

1. Lilian Katz, "The Project Approach," Pamphlet EDO–PS–94–6 (Educational Resource and Information Center [ERIC], 1994), nonpaginated.

2. M. C. Feinstein and T. L. Veenendall, "Using the Case Study Method to Teach Interpersonal Communication," *INQUIRY: Critical Thinking Across the Disciplines*, vol. 9, no. 3 (Institute for Critical Thinking, April 1992), p. 11.

3. Sally Smith, "Educating the Learning Disabled for the Future," *Their World* (National Center for Learning Disabilities, 1992), p. 17.

4. "The CoVis Project Pedagogy," http://www.covis.nwn.edu/Geosciences/philosophy/philosophy.html.

5. George Balich, referenced by Arli Quesada in "The Boston Community Comes to the Aid of Don Bocso Preparatory," *Education by Design* (Autodesk Foundation, Winter, 1997), pp. 8–9.

6. Michael B. Eisenberg and Robert E. Berkowitz, "The Six Study Habits of Highly Effective Students: Using the Big Six to Link Parents, Students, and Homework," *School Library Journal*, vol. 41, no. 8 (August 1995), p. 24.

7. "Project Design Process," developed by Ross Valley School District, San Anselmo, California, in collaboration with Autodesk Foundation, www.autodesk.com/foundation.

8. Alfie Kohn, "Choices for Children: Why and How to Let Students Decide," *Phi Delta Kappan*, vol. 75, no. 1 (September 1993), p. 13.

9. Nora Redding, "Assessing the Big Outcomes," *Educational Leadership*, vol. 49, no. 8 (Association for Supervision and Curriculum Development, May 1992), p. 53.

10. Tom Ostlund, 1992, referenced by David Haury and Peter Rillero in "Perspectives of Hands-On Science Teaching," (ERIC Clearinghouse for Science, Mathematics and Environmental Education, 1994), p. 32.

11. Keith Beery, *Teamwork!* (2830 Heatherstone Drive, San Rafael, Calif. 94903, 1997), p. 9.

12. Daniel Goleman, *Emotional Intelligence* (New York: Bantam Books, 1995), p. 276.

13. Alfie Kohn, "Choices for Children: Why and How to Let Students Decide," *Phi Delta Kappan*, vol. 75, no. 1 (September 1993), pp. 15–16.

14. David Haury and Peter Rillero in "Perspectives of Hands-On Science Teaching" (ERIC Clearinghouse for Science, Mathematics and Environmental Education, 1994), p. 32.

15. Terry Thode as quoted by Arli Quesada in "A Mind Set for the Future," *The Technology Teacher* (International Technology Education Association, October 1995), p. 4.

16. Wendy Oxman, "Critical Thinking as Creativity," *INQUIRY: Critical Thinking Across the Disciplines*, vol. 9, no. 3 (Institute for Critical Thinking, April 1992), p. 1.

17. "Project-Based Learning: An Effective Approach" (Global School Net Foundation), cdweb@gsn.org.

18. Keith Beery, *Teamwork!* (2830 Heatherstone Drive, San Rafael, Calif. 94903, 1997), p. 44.

Next Steps: Integrating Media Literacy into Our Schools and Communities

1. Kendall Starkweather, International Technology Education Association (ITEA) keynote address at Autodesk Foundation's Midwinter Conference on Project-Based Education, 1994.

GLOSSARY

America Online. Computer service accessible from a home computer using a modem; provides users with e-mail, chat rooms, home shopping, audiovisual material.

analyze. To examine in detail; breaking the whole into parts to examine its nature.

animation. The art of making drawings move. A video made up of individual frames of graphic art, such as computer-generated images.

audience. Those gathered to hear or see something. Those reached by the radio, a book, TV programs, etc.

author. One who makes or creates something. The writer of a book, producer of a show, etc.

BBC. The British Broadcasting Corporation; the United Kingdom's government-sanctioned television service. The BBC is paid for by the viewers through fees charged to everyone who owns a TV.

brainstorming. To engage in discussion with the intent of producing ideas.

broadcast television. TV stations that transmit (broadcast) their TV programs over the airwaves. ABC, CBS, FOX, and NBC are broadcast networks. Even if you are receiving these networks over a cable system, they are still considered broadcast television because the original signal was broadcast.

cable television. Television that uses cables to transmit programs to the home. The Cable News Network (CNN), Cable Satellite Public Affairs Network (C-SPAN), Showtime, and Home Box Office (HBO) are examples of networks and program services received via cable.

captions. Printed explanations of the pictures that appear on-screen.

CATV. Community Antenna Television.

CD. A compact disc storing digital information that is retrieved by a low-power laser beam; made of iridescent plastic.

CD-ROM. A compact disk storing acoustic and visual information; used with personal computers; ROM stands for "read-only memory."

celebrity. A well-known person, animal, or character.

censorship. The act of banning anything regarded as harmful. Examination for the purpose of removal.

CNN. Cable News Network, a major commercial cable network.

commercial. An advertising message on a television station. The message attempts to influence the viewer to buy a certain product.

community. A body of people living in one place or district who consider themselves a whole. A group with common interests or origins.

construct. To make by placing parts together; to build.

constructivist. An approach to pedagogy based on the belief that learning is constructed.

credits. A list of those who contributed to a production. Credits are usually shown at the end of the production.

cyberspace. The world of the Internet and online services and everything available online.

DAT. Digital audiotape; a recording medium that stores digital information.

DBS. Direct broadcast satellite; a satellite that broadcasts signals directly to an Earth-based satellite dish.

deconstruct. To take apart; to analyze the individual parts to better understand the whole.

democracy. Government by the whole people of a country through representatives whom they elect.

desktop publishing. The use of personal computers to format text and graphics for publication.

digital. Information reduced to a binary form of ones and zeros or on/off. Once information is converted to a digital form, it can be manipulated, stored, and used by computers as well as transmitted by a variety of media.

digitization. The process of encoding previously formatted information such as video or sound into a digital medium.

director. The individual who directs the action for the production and makes final decisions regarding the creative responsibilities of production.

documentary. An explanation of a topic taken directly from documentary evidence. A good documentary adheres to factual information about the topic.

editorial. An article giving the editor's comments on current affairs.

e-mail. Electronic mail; computers, telephone lines, and/or communication satellites are used to transmit messages between computers, rather than using the postal system to deliver paper-based messages.

evaluate. To assess, find out, state, or judge the value of something.

executive producer. The individual with overall control of a production. This individual overseeing the producer, director, and editor.

fact. Something known to have happened, to be true, or to exist.

FCC. The Federal Communication Commission. A government agency that regulates the television broadcasting and cable industry as well as other national telecommunications.

feedback. An act of communication from the receiver of a message to the sender of that message; the sender interprets the feedback to assess the impact of the original message.

fiction. A product of the imagination, an invented story, or a class of literature consisting of such stories.

format. The basic programming style of a radio station, such as classic rock, urban contemporary, talk radio, and so on.

FTC. The Federal Trade Commission. A government agency that regulates misleading advertising.

gatekeeper. An individual or group that controls the flow of information or entertainment. The gatekeeper can select, delete, or reorganize information. Example of a gatekeeper is a managing editor of a newspaper.

HBO. Home Box Office, a commercial cable service primarily offering movies.

hero/heroine. A person who is admired for brave or noble deeds; the lead character in a story, play, or poem.

home page. *See* website.

HTML. Hypertext Markup Language. The basic webpage instructions that enable documents containing images, text, and other elements to be displayed by browsers.

hyperlinks. Highlighted words or pictures that you can click on so you can instantly travel to another web document.

hypertext. A system by which users can move from site to site around the Internet by means of hyperlinks. Using these links, a user can hop around the Internet, connecting to a variety of sites around a topic of interest.

inappropriate language. Profanity, hate language, racial slurs, put-downs, or negative slang.

interactive/interactivity. Ways for people to interplay with multimedia products and online environments. Interactivity allows people to select information, modify elements like music, participate in real-time online video conferences, make choices, and receive information in response to their questions or choices.

interactive television. Programming, video games, etc. that run on television sets and in which the viewer is a participant.

Internet. The global network of computer networks composed of commercial online services, university computer networks, and government computer networks; the infrastructure of cyberspace.

IQ. Intelligence quotient.

Kidvid. Refers to TV programming aimed specifically at children. Kidvid commercials are ads meant to be aired on Saturday morning or during other children's programming.

leader. The head of the group; the one whose example is followed.

literacy. The state of being able to read and write. In media literacy, refers to ability to "read" (deconstruct and decipher meaning of) and "write" (create or produce) media messages.

marketing. A broad term for activity in support of product sales and distribution.

mass communication. One-way communication from a central source to a mass of people simultaneously.

mass media. A communications medium capable of reaching a mass of people simultaneously, something through or by which something is accomplished, conveyed, or carried on.

media. Literally, the plural of *medium*. In media literacy, can refer to a mixed group of print and electronic communications such as newspapers, TV, and the Internet. In common usage, the term *media* is sometimes used to reference all types of mass media.

media elements. Words, images, and other means of expressing ideas or information.

media literacy. The combination of knowledge and skills required to access, analyze, interpret, evaluate, and create media in a variety of forms.

media product. Any single item from a given medium, such as a book, magazine, TV show, CD, or Internet site.

medium. Plural: media. A channel or system of communication or expression. To a communication specialist, television is a medium; to an artist, chalk is a medium; to a sculptor, clay is a medium.

message. Communication via verbal, print, electronic, or other means. To have accomplished, conveyed, or carried on something.

metacognitive. Becoming aware of or considering the process of your own thinking.

modem. A device that hooks a personal computer to a telephone line. Modems transmit and receive computer files through telephone lines.

monopoly. The control of a market or a commodity by a single owner, which restrains competition.

motivational research. The study of what motivates consumers to buy or not buy certain products and brands. The focus in this kind of research is on the "why" of behavior.

multimedia. Traditional or new media forms of communication that combine text, music, video, photos, art, and/or animation. New media comes in the form of a CD–ROM or other electronic media; often highly interactive.

negative. A "no" statement; against, opposed to; distrusting or unhopeful opinion or personal belief.

network. A media company that obtains and distributes programming to affiliated stations or cable systems for transmission to consumers.

new media. Form of communication that can combine text, music, video, photos, art, and animation. CD–ROM or other electronic media; often highly interactive.

online service. Commercial information service accessible by home computer and modem for which subscribers pay monthly or hourly fees; examples include America Online, Prodigy, and CompuServe.

opinion. Someone's thoughts or feelings about what they believe in their own mind to be true.

PBS. Public Broadcasting Service. A nonprofit television network.

PC. Personal computer. Portable computers designed for use in an office, at home, or at school.

Point of view (POV). The way in which one looks at various subject matters. In film, the perspective from which the filmmaker decides to shoot a film.

pop culture. The totality of widely popular media products such as contemporary music, mass market paperbacks, prime-time television shows, mass circulation magazines, and so on.

positive. A "yes" statement; favorable, supportive, trusting, or hopeful opinion or personal belief.

prime time. The times during which television has its largest adult audience: 8:00 to 11:00 P.M.

producer. The individual who puts the entire production together, including budgeting, hiring, and overall planning.

Public Service Announcement (PSA). Announcement on television or radio for charitable or other worthwhile endeavors presented free of charge by broadcasters.

rating. The percentage of all TV households tuned to a particular program. A rating of 22 means that 22 percent of all TV households were tuned in to the same program.

receiver. The person receiving information in the act of communication.

script. Written narration or dialogue. Usually also contains detailed instructions regarding the production.

sender. The person or entity initiating an act of communication.

sitcoms. Situation comedies. Television shows.

society. An organized community and the system of living in a community.

sound effects. Honks, beeps, screeches, and other sounds that accompany films, television shows, and electronic media.

special effects. The technical manipulation of graphics, pictures, sounds, etc. to create a visual or alter its effect.

spot. The time used for a single commercial or announcement.

station. A radio or television facility that broadcasts on a particular channel in a particular area.

stereotype. An oversimplified description based on limited experience. TV shows often use stereotyped characters who are instantly recognizable by viewers.

storyboard. A scene–by–scene depiction of the story, including detailed sketches with notes about voice–overs, sound effects, and other media elements that accompany the scene.

survey. A way to find out information about a subject by asking people a series of questions, usually in the form of a questionnaire, about their thoughts, preferences, and activities.

target audience. The group of viewers toward whom a particular program, commercial, or advertisement is directed.

target marketing. Programming or advertising aimed at a specific age, ethnic, income, or otherwise defined group.

technical director. The individual who supervises the technical work.

transfer. To apply information and understanding from one arena to another.

videocamera. A camera that reproduces images using videotape; a new technology tool.

violence. An action involving great force, strength, or intensity with intent to injure.

virtual reality (VR). Computer–generated environment meant to simulate a realistic or fantasy environment.

visual medium. A medium where pictures are the primary way to communicate. Film and television are examples.

voice–over. An audio recording of someone's voice. In a documentary, the voice of the narrator. In an animation, the voice of the characters.

website. Also known as "webpage." A place on the Internet where text, audio, graphic, and animated information reside.

WebTV. An electronic, pay–per–view device that allows users to connect to the Internet via the television.

World Wide Web (WWW). Also known as the "web." A global, hypertext information system on the Internet.

BIBLIOGRAPHY

Arnold, Arnold. *Violence and Your Child*. Chicago: Henry Regnery Company, 1969.

Beery, Keith. *Teamwork!* San Rafael, Calif., 1997: pp. 9, 44.

Berger, Larry, Dahlia Lithwick, and Steven Campers. *I Will Sing Life*. Boston: Little, Brown, 1992.

Black, Kaye. *KidVid*. Tucson, Ariz.: Zephyr Press, 1989.

Burke, James. Keynote speaker, Apple New Media Forum, June 15, 1995.

Chaffee, John. "Critical Thinking Skills: The Cornerstone of Developmental Education." *Journal of Developmental Education*, vol. 15, no. 3. (Spring 1992): p. 2.

Chen, Milton. *The Smart Parent's Guide to KIDS' TV*. San Francisco: KQED Books, 1994.

Clinton, Hillary Rodham. *It Takes a Village: And Other Lessons Children Teach Us*. New York: Simon & Schuster, 1996.

Cole, Jeffrey, principal investigator. *The UCLA Television Violence Monitoring Report*. Los Angeles: UCLA Center for Communication Policy, September 1995.

Considine, David M. "An Introduction to Media Literacy: The What, Why and How To's." *Telemedium, The Journal of Media Literacy*, vol. 41, no. 2 (Fall 1995).

Costa, Arthur L., and Bena Kallick, eds. *Assessment in the Learning Organization: Shifting the Paradigm*. Alexandria, Va.: Association for Supervision and Curriculum Development, 1995.

"The CoVis Project Pedagogy," http://www.covis.nwn.edu/Geosciences/philosophy/philosophy.html.

Debar, Ron. *Returning Light to the Wind*. Waterloo, Ont.: Windmill Press, 1995.

Duncan, Barry, Janine D'Ippolito, Cam Macpherson, and Carolyn Wilson, eds. *Mass Media and Popular Culture*. Toronto: Harcourt, Brace, 1996.

Edelman, Marian Wright. *The Measure of Our Success: A Letter to My Children and Yours*. Boston: Beacon Press, 1992.

Edwards, Carolyn, Lella Gandini, and George Forman, eds. *The Hundred Languages of Children: The Reggio Emilia Approach to Early Childhood Education.* Norwood, N.J.: Ablex Publishing, 1993.

Eisenberg, Michael B., and Robert E. Berkowitz. "The Six Study Habits of Highly Effective Students: Using the Big Six to Link Parents, Students, and Homework." *School Library Journal,* vol. 41, no. 8 (August 1995): p. 24.

English-Language Arts Framework. Sacramento: California Department of Education, 1987.

Feinstein, M. C., and T. L. Veenendall. "Using the Case Study Method to Teach Interpersonal Communication." *INQUIRY: Critical Thinking Across the Disciplines,* vol. 9, no. 3 (Institute for Critical Thinking April 1992): p. 11.

Ferguson, Donald, and Jim Patten, eds. *Journalism Today!* Lincolnwood, Ill.: National Textbook Company, 1993.

Foreign Language Framework. Sacramento: California Department of Education, 1996.

Fox, Roy. *Harvesting Minds: How TV Commercials Control Kids.* Westport, Conn.: Praeger Publishers, 1996.

The Framework Focus: Answers to Key Questions About Implementation of the English-Language Arts Framework. Sacramento: California Department of Education, 1994.

Fullan, Michael. *Change Forces: Probing the Depths of Educational Reform.* Philadelphia: Falmer Press, 1993.

Gaetz, Jamie, ed. *The Overview '96: Productions for Children and Young People.* Montreal: International Center for Films for Children and Young People, 1996.

Gerbner, George. *Women and Minorities on Television: A Study in Casting and Fate.* Report to the Screen Actors Guild and the American Federation of Radio and Television Artists. Philadelphia, June 1993.

Glatthorn, Allan. *Developing a Quality Curriculum.* Alexandria, Va.: Association for Supervision and Curriculum Development, 1994.

Goleman, Daniel. *Emotional Intelligence.* New York: Bantam Books, 1995.

Grunebaum, L. H. *Philosophy for Modern Man: A Popular Survey.* New York: Horizon Press, 1970.

Halliburton, Warren. *Historic Speeches of African Americans.* New York: Franklin Watts, 1993.

Harvard Educational Review, special issue: *Violence and Youth,* vol. 65, no. 2 (Summer 1995).

Haury, David, and Peter Rillero. "Perspectives of Hands–On Science Teaching." (ERIC Clearinghouse for Science, Mathematics and Environmental Education, 1994).

Hazen, Don, and Larry Smith, eds. *Free the Media.* New York: New Press, 1997.

Health Framework for California Public Schools Kindergarten Through Grade Twelve. Sacramento: California Department of Education, 1994.

Healy, Jane. *Endangered Minds: Why Our Children Don't Think and What We Can Do About It.* New York: Simon & Schuster, 1990.

Heiferman, Marvin, and Carole Kismaric. *Talking Pictures: People Speak About the Photographs That Speak to Them.* San Francisco: Chronicle Books, 1994.

History—Social Welfare Framework. Sacramento: California Department of Education, 1988.

Jacobson, Michael, and Laurie Ann Mazur. *Marketing Madness: A Survival Guide for a Consumer Society.* Boulder, Colo.: Westview Press, 1995.

Jawitz, William, ed. *Understanding Mass Media*, 5th ed. Lincolnwood, Ill.: National Textbook Company, 1996.

Katz, Lilian. "The Project Approach," Pamphlet EDO–PS–94–6. (Educational Resource and Information Center, ERIC, 1994).

Kohn, Alfie. "Choices for Children: Why and How to Let Students Decide," *Phi Delta Kappan*, vol. 75, issue 1 (September 1993): pp. 13, 15–16.

Lewis, Shari, and Barrett Robert. *One-Minute Stories of Great Americans.* New York: Doubleday, 1990.

Maestro, Betsy, and Guilio Maestro. *The Voice of the People: American Democracy in Action.* New York: Lothrop, Lee & Shepard, 1996.

Margulies, Nancy. *Yes, You Can ... Draw! An Interactive Guide Book for Learners.* Bucks, U.K.: Accelerated Learning Systems, 1991.

McChesney, Robert. *Telecommunications, Mass Media, & Democracy: The Battle for Control of U.S. Broadcasting, 1928–1935.* New York: Oxford University Press, 1994.

McLeod, Michael, producer. *Frontline:* "Does TV Kill?" (video). Boston: WGBH TV, 1987.

McLuhan, Marshall. *Understanding Media: The Extensions of Man.* New York: McGraw–Hill, 1964.

Menzel, Peter. *Material World: A Global Family Portrait.* San Francisco: Sierra Club Books, 1994.

O'Reilly, Kevin, and John Splaine. *Critical Viewing: Stimulant to Critical Thinking.* Pacific Grove, Calif.: Critical Thinking Press and Software, 1996.

Oxman, Wendy. "Critical Thinking as Creativity." *INQUIRY: Critical Thinking Across the Disciplines*, vol. 9, no. 3 (Institute for Critical Thinking, April 1992): p. 2.

Paul, Richard. *Critical Thinking: How to Prepare Students for a Rapidly Changing World.* Santa Rosa, Calif.: Foundation for Critical Thinking, 1995.

Pearce, Joseph Chilton. *Evolution's End: Claiming the Potential of Our Intelligence.* New York: HarperCollins, 1992.

Postman, Neil. *Amusing Ourselves to Death: Public Discourse in the Age of Show Business.* New York: Elisabeth Sifton Books, 1986.

———. *The End of Education.* New York: Alfred A. Knopf, 1995.

"Project-Based Learning: An Effective Approach" (Global School Net Foundation, 1995).

"Project Design Process," developed by Ross Valley School District, San Anselmo, California, in collaboration with Autodesk Foundation, www.autodesk.com/foundation.

Quesada, Arli. "The Boston Community Comes to the Aid of Don Bocso Preparatory," *Education by Design.* Autodesk Foundation (Winter 1997): pp. 8–9.

———. "A Mind Set for the Future," *The Technology Teacher.* International Technology Education Association (October 1995): p. 4.

Redding, Nora. "Assessing the Big Outcomes," *Educational Leadership* (Association for Supervision and Curriculum Development, May 1992).

Silverblatt, Art. *Media Literacy: Keys to Interpreting Media Messages.* Westport, Conn.: Praeger Publishers, 1995.

Singer, Dorothy, Jerome Singer, and Diana Zuckerman. *Teaching Television: How to Use TV to Your Children's Advantage.* New York: Dial Press, 1981.

Smith, Sally. "Education the Learning Disabled for the Future," *Their World* (National Center for Learning Disabilities, 1992): p. 17.

Southam Interactive. *Understanding McLuhan.* New York: Voyager Company, 1996.

Splaine, John, and Pam Splaine. *Educating the Consumer of Television: An Interactive Approach.* Pacific Grove, Calif.: Critical Thinking Press and Software, 1992.

Starkweather, Kendall. International Technology Education Association (ITEA) keynote address at Autodesk Foundation's Midwinter Conference on Project-Based Education, 1994.

Streeter, Thomas. *Selling the Air.* Chicago: University of Chicago Press, 1996.

Summers, Sue Lockwood. *Media Alert! 200 Activities to Create Media-Savvy Kids.* Littleton, Colo.: Media Alert! Publishers, 2000.

Thomas, Paulette. "Show and Tell: Advertisers Take Pitches to Preschools," *The Wall Street Journal* (October 28, 1996): pp. B1, B5.

Valenti, Jack. *Ratings Roundtable*, 1996.

Visual and Performing Arts Framework. Sacramento: California Board of Education, 1996.

Walsh, David, Ph.D. *Selling Out America's Children.* Minneapolis: Fairview Press, 1994.

Walsh David, Ph.D., Larry S. Goldman, Ph.D., and Roger Brown, Ph.D. *Physician Guide to Media Violence.* Chicago: American Medical Association, 1996.

Watson Jr., Thomas, and Peter Petre. *Father, Son & Co.: My Life at IBM and Beyond.* New York: Bantam Books, 1990.

Webster's New World Dictionary, Third College Edition. Victoria Neufeldt, ed. New York: Simon & Schuster, 1988.

Williams, Linda Verlee. *Teaching for the Two-Sided Mind.* New York: Simon & Schuster, 1983.

Willis–Braithwaite, Deborah. *VanDerZee Photographer 1886–1983.* New York: Harry N. Abrams, 1993.

Wilson, Leslie Owen. *Every Child, Whole Child: Classroom Activities for Unleashing Natural Abilites.* Tuscon, Ariz.: Zephyr Press, 1994.

Wilson, Stephen. *World Wide Web Design Guide.* Indianapolis: Hayden Books, 1995.

Wright, June L., and Daniel D. Shade. *Young Children: Active Learners in a Technological Age.* Washington, D.C.: National Association for the Education of Young Children, 1994.

Wurman, Richard Saul. *Information Anxiety: What to Do When Information Doesn't Tell You What You Need to Know.* New York: Bantam Books, 1989.

INDEX

ABOUT THE AUTHORS

Elana Yonah Rosen has fifteen years of experience in the nonprofit and media worlds, having worked with KQED-TV in the news, current affairs, and cultural departments. She then joined the George Lucas Educational Foundation, where she developed educational interactive prototypes, produced the content for dramatic films on future learning environments, and created a national information resource for dissemination on the Internet.

Rosen has lectured on multimedia, online information, and educational issues at various institutions including Stanford University, Santa Clara University, and Mills College. In 1995 she produced an interactive exhibition for the 50th anniversary of the United Nations and has consulted with educational software companies such as Tenth Planet and Living Books. She received an Emmy nomination for the documentary "Czeslaw Milosz: A Poet Remembers."

Arleta (Arli) Paulin Quesada has more than ten years of experience in the field of educational publishing, working with both print and software companies. She was developmental editor of one of the first interactive CD-ROM teacher's guides, the *Multimedia Cookbook for HyperStudio®*, and the author of the "Integrated Learning Activities" in the teacher's guide to the *1998 Grolier Multimedia Encyclopedia*, published by the Learning Company. Previously, she worked for Academic Therapy Publications, publisher of learning materials for students with special needs.

Quesada, a freelance author who specializes in education and technology, has written articles for *Technology & Learning* and *Converge* magazines, and for *The Technology Teacher*, the journal of the International Technology Education Association.

Sue Lockwood Summers is a library media specialist in an elementary school near Denver, Colorado, and is a member of the Turner Learning National Faculty.

Summers serves on the board of PRIIME TIIME TODAY (Parents Responsibly Involved In Media Excellence and Teens Involved In Media Excellence), which conducts an annual statewide media literacy essay contest for high school students.

She has developed and teaches two University of Northern Colorado graduate courses related to the media for teachers, and she is the author of *Media Alert! 200 Activities to Create Media-Savvy Kids*, which introduces teachers, parents, and community workers to media literacy activities.

Summers can be contacted at <CNFSueLS@aol.com>.